PRAEGER LIBRARY OF AFRICAN AFFAIRS
CHRISTIANITY AND THE NEW AFRICA

The Praeger Library of African Affairs is intended to provide clear, objective, and authoritative information about the historical, political, cultural, and economic background of modern Africa. Individual countries and groupings of countries will be dealt with, as will general themes affecting the whole continent and its relations with the rest of the world. The library appears under the general editorship of Colin Legum, and each volume is written by an acknowledged expert on its subject.

T. A. Beetham

CHRISTIANITY AND
THE NEW AFRICA

FREDERICK A. PRAEGER, *Publishers*

New York · Washington · London

FREDERICK A. PRAEGER, INC., *Publishers*
111 Fourth Avenue, New York, N.Y. 10003, U.S.A.
77-79 Charlotte Street, London, W.1, England

Published in the United States of America in 1967
by Frederick A. Praeger, Inc., Publishers

Library of Congress Catalog Card Number: 67-14705

PRINTED IN GREAT BRITAIN

*To the Staff and
Students of Wesley College, Kumasi,
of the years 1928–1948*

Contents

Contents

Preface

RECENTLY, I spent an evening in Dakar with a pastor from Cameroon and a teacher and his wife from Togo. The conversation ranged wide and late, but it came back time and again to Africa's sense of community and of the oneness of the spiritual and material. Here, it was claimed, in the social and religious sphere, Africa had a contribution to make to the West. Any of the three African Christians present that evening could write more vitally than I on 'Christianity and the new Africa'. The main reason for an observer from Europe attempting such a theme today is that there are as yet not many Africans with a wide geographical knowledge of their continent. That, and a working life related to the Church in Africa, are my reasons for attempting this survey. Even so, I am aware that what I set out to do has been very unevenly performed. Lack of time for a comprehensive study of documents and reports has meant that I have had to rely too much on personal experience and contacts; hence anglophone Africa outweighs francophone; West Africa outweighs the East and South; Protestant outweighs Catholic; and Britain outweighs the European continent and America. (Generally speaking, I use the terms 'Protestant' and 'Catholic' without qualification, in accordance with 'popular

[ix]

usage', to designate the two main groups in Western Christendom.)

Because this book points to the many problems facing the Church in Africa today, African readers may be left with the feeling that the problems they face are different from those facing Christians in other parts of the world. I should be sorry if that were so, for parallel illustrations could be given from Europe and America, from Asia and Latin America. The basic problem of the relevance of the Christian faith to the contemporary situation faces the Church of every country. Those who tackle the issues within Africa do so in a world setting.

I have refrained from attempting to name individually the many to whom I am indebted in the gathering of material and the preparation of the final text of this book. In an area in which statistics are not readily available, a number of correspondents, particularly secretaries of Christian Councils, have responded generously to my requests for figures. My summary of past history owes its starting point to Professor C. P. Groves' *The Planting of Christianity in Africa*. To all who have thus helped me, my thanks are gratefully offered.

I have dedicated the book to those with whom I used to live in a college community in Ghana because it was they who, in so many ways, direct and indirect, helped someone of the colonial era to begin to prepare his mind for the new Africa.

T. A. BEETHAM

Selsdon, Surrey
December 1966

MAPS

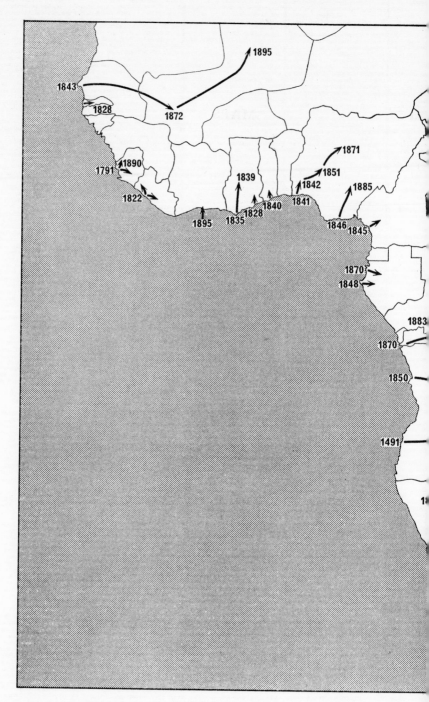

1. PENETRATION OF CHRISTIANITY IN SUB-SAHARAN AFRICA UP TO 1900

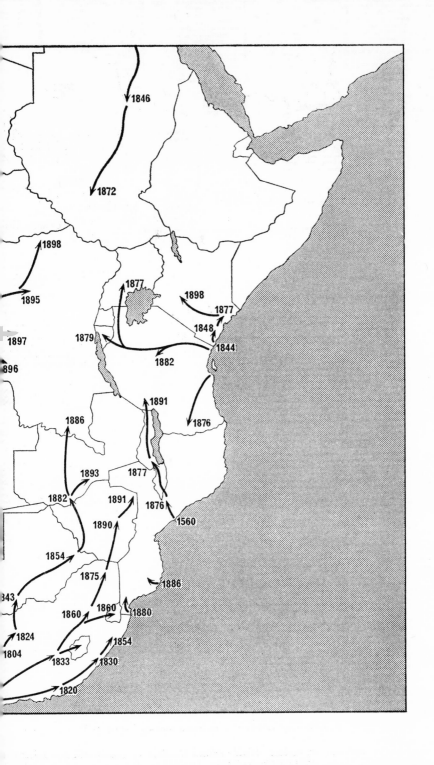

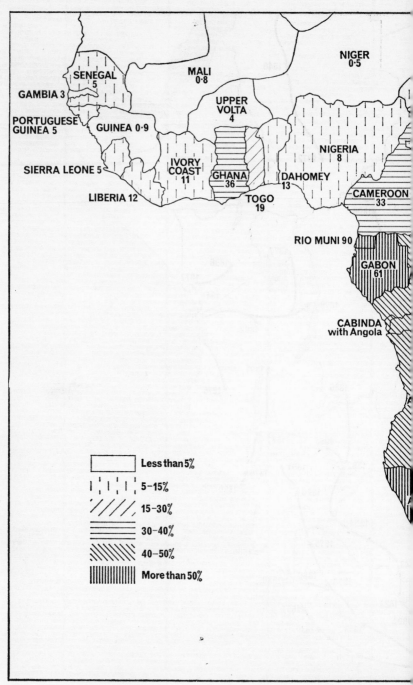

2. CHRISTIAN COMMUNITY IN SUB-SAHARAN AFRICA AS PERCENTAGE OF POPULATION

Sources: Protestant—*World Christian Handbook 1962*, corrected and adjusted 1964 population figures
Catholic—*Herder Correspondence*, July 1966, based on 1964 figures

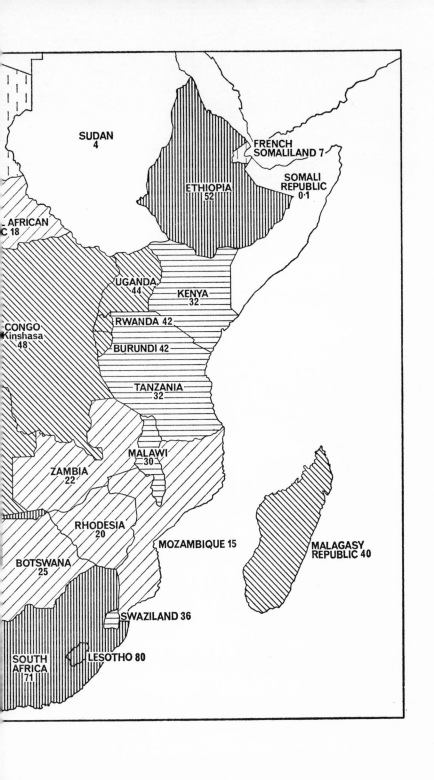

CHRISTIANITY AND THE NEW AFRICA

I

The Question Posed

IN A SMALL TOWN some twenty miles from the coast in Ghana
is a village church, its thick mud-built walls nearly a hundred
years old. That it is Methodist, and not Roman Catholic or
Anglican or Presbyterian, is immaterial. Seventy years ago
Aggrey of Achimota was a pupil teacher in the school that met
in the church on weekdays. Twenty years earlier Sir Garnet
Wolseley camped in the nearby resthouse during the British
campaign against Ashanti of 1873–4. You do not see the church
as you go through the town by car today; the modern motor-
road has passed it by; it sits beside the old forest path where for
many years the church and the resthouse marked the entrance
to the village. What you see instead are cement-block buildings
of the modern school flanking the motor-road, direct successor
to the school where Aggrey taught. Are these three buildings—
the old church, the old resthouse, the new school—a parable?
Most of the resthouses that marked the night's camp and court-
house of the District Commissioner, essence and symbol of
colonial rule, are crumbling; white ants and tropical vegetation
quickly overwhelm them. Will the church be the next to meet
the same fate? Was it, also, merely the symbol of a passing
phenomenon of the colonial era, gaining what strength it had

from its prestige as representing the religion of the foreign rulers? Can that religion continue in the face of Nationalism, Islam, Secularism? Or will it come to be remembered as an incident of the 1870s to 1970s, worth a place in history as the initial inspiration and provider of the educational system of modern Africa, but significant simply as an event of the past and no more?

Viewed solely as an historical event, the full significance of that one church building must not be underestimated: a hundred years of African pastors' making their home in the single-storey mission house across the path from the church; a fellowship of men and women, albeit only a proportion of the total population of the town, in whose lives Christian worship on Sunday mornings was a reality, and who came back to the church on Sunday afternoons to learn to read, so that they could read the New Testament for themselves in their homes; the tradition set by the minister, and repeated in the homes of the leaders, of family prayer just before daybreak, before the compound gate was opened, the compound swept, the water fetched and the day's work begun. On the Sunday morning in 1961 when the Methodist Church of Ghana, for long internally self-governing, celebrated the attainment of full autonomous status, a native of the town who was back home for the weekend worshipped in that small old church. He had many years of courageous newspaper editing to his credit; both British colonial and Ghanaian national governments had in their time reproved him for what he regarded as fair comment on public issues. His contribution to the well-being of society owed much not only to the education that church school gave him as a boy but to the continuing fellowship through the years of the Church into whose faith as an infant he had been baptised.

This is but a glimpse into the largely unrecorded history of that one small town church: a glimpse which suggests that its influence is not to be lightly weighed. What concerns us now is whether this fellowship of Christians, as a worshipping community and as activating leaven in society, will continue in post-independent Africa. This is a deeper, more fundamental, question than whether a new cathedral will be built alongside the modern school buildings by the motor-road to replace that back-street mud chapel.

Have the roots of the Christian community gone sufficiently deep in African society, with its traditional belief in the Supreme God and the spirit-world, its ritual for purification and consequent protection of individuals from harm within the family and clan? Has it a continuing place in that society as it now responds to the joint demands of nationalism and bureaucratic technology? In the life of the new Africa, much changed already from both pre-colonial and colonial days, and bound to change still more radically during the next twenty years, is Christianity an appendage, a hangover from the past? Has it been 'merely a transitory stage, a brief stop-over between animism and secularism'?[1] Or is it relevant to the struggle of Africans to build their nations on a sound basis of economic and social development? May the Christian faith become increasingly a living interpretation and fulfilment of African spirituality?

In the following pages we shall attempt to look at these questions in the countries of Africa south of the Sahara as part of a single question of world-wide significance: the relevance of the Christian faith to modern secular man. In the context of European society, the questions asked above call just as urgently for an answer. That back-street chapel in West Africa is still today a place of worship; its counterpart in a small Yorkshire hamlet has just been pulled down, and in the inner belt of Manchester or London many such chapels have become furniture depositories: a fate that other consecrated buildings were spared by the intervention of incendiary bombs. In its religious quest, and in its question mark against the validity of the Christian faith, the world is one.

To attempt an answer within the geographical limits set, it will be necessary first to examine the state of the Christian Church in Africa at the point of national independence. This in its turn requires a preliminary study of the manner in which the Gospel came to be proclaimed in Africa.

2

The Coming of Christianity to Africa

THE OLDEST CHURCH in the African continent, the Ethiopian Orthodox Church dates from the fourth century; yet it seems to have exerted no direct influence on, nor taken part in any extension of the Christian faith to, the rest of the continent. Only since 1960 has there been fellowship between the Ethiopian Church and Churches elsewhere in Africa. There was in the nineteenth century one indirect influence: the knowledge that there existed a completely African Church in Ethiopia, taken with the words of Psalm 68, 'Ethiopia shall soon stretch out her hands unto God', inspired those who founded the early Independent Churches of Southern Africa as they sought for themselves a worshipping community free of white overlordship.

For the source of the expansion of Christianity to Africa south of the Sahara we have therefore to look, not to North-east Africa, but to Europe, and later North America. The first European missionaries were Portuguese, bringing the Gospel at a time when Western Christians were still undivided and all owed allegiance to the See of Rome. In the explorations along the African coast during the fifteenth century under Prince Henry the Navigator, priests generally accompanied the expeditions.

They served as chaplains to the new trading settlements and as missionaries to neighbouring African peoples. By 1500, the Gospel had been preached at the courts of the kingdoms of Benin and Congo, in one case with immediate response from members of the royal family. A son of the king of Congo became a priest after receiving training in Portugal, and was elevated to a bishopric in 1518. By the mid-seventeenth century the Jesuits had established a monastery in San Paulo de Loanda which by then had superseded the capital of Congo, San Salvador, as an ecclesiastical centre. On the other side of the continent, Portuguese Jesuits had pushed their way inland from the mouth of the Zambesi into what is now Rhodesia. Their first missionary priest was martyred in 1561, some 600 miles from the Zambesi mouth, but a later paramount chief was baptised by the Dominicans in 1652.

All these missions, some of them gaining congregations of real strength, had faded away almost completely by the end of the eighteenth century. Among the reasons advanced for this failure are: the alliance of the Portuguese with the overseas slave trade; the political effect on missionary policy of the patronal rights of the Portuguese crown; the difficulty of training African priests in Europe and the absence of any seminary in Africa; the smallness of the effective cadre of missionaries, whose efficiency and numbers were continually reduced by climate and disease; and, at the end of the period, the setback in Europe successively experienced through the expulsion of the Jesuits from Portugal and elsewhere, the anti-clericalism of the French Revolution and Napoleon's actions against the Pope.

When, therefore, a new missionary movement to Africa began at the end of the eighteenth century—this time initiated by Protestant Churches and as a direct result of the evangelical revival in Europe—traces of the previous Catholic movement were almost non-existent. There were a few ruined walls, a crucifix among the sacred objects of a local shrine, and faint memories in tradition of a god who died. There had already been on the Protestant side a comparatively small development of settlement chaplaincies parallel with, though rather later than, the Catholic ones. By the middle of the seventeenth century, chaplains were (if intermittently) part of the staff of the Danes at Christiansborg, the British at Cape Coast, the Dutch at Elmina and the Cape of Good Hope. They, too, had occasionally reached out beyond the confines of the trading settlement to the local population, but with little effect—perhaps because of little conviction. Significantly, the one outreach with permanent results in this period, that from the Cape, was through missionaries of another agency and not from the chaplaincy Church itself. Was unreceptiveness to the arguments against the slave trade which were inherent in their faith as much a factor with the Protestants before the end of the eighteenth century as with Catholics? It may well have been, for the Protestant advances into Africa at the close of that century were closely linked, in West Africa, with the Christian groups among the freed slaves in Sierra Leone, and, in the missionary societies in Britain, with just that element in British religious life which was engaged in fighting the slave trade in Parliament. When the renewed Roman Catholic approach came to be made a little later, it is on record that 'Cardinal Lavigerie both founded an African mission and headed an anti-slavery crusade'.[1] This may have something to say to the Church of the 1960s in those areas where Europeans still desire to maintain a mental, social and economic domination, if no longer with physical shackles.

★

The modern planting of the Church in Africa may be said to begin with the non-white settlers from the ex-slave areas of the New World who were settled at Freetown in Sierra Leone from 1791 onwards. To the several consecutive waves of these ex-slaves were added during the next fifty years the cargoes of slave ships captured along the West Coast by the British Navy and set free in Freetown harbour. The roofing timbers of a church at York on the Freetown peninsula all come from one such slave ship; the central pillars are still unmistakably sections of the masts. The first Negro settlers—from Nova Scotia, Jamaica and England—were already Christians before their return to the continent of their fathers. They were members of various Protestant denominations: Anglicans, Baptists, Methodists, Countess of Huntingdon's Connexion. Those with a tradition of lay preachers had such among them on arrival. In their new home they built their churches and chapels, and continued to worship according to their various traditions under the leadership of their lay preachers, except for the Anglicans for whom the Sierra Leone Company provided a chaplain from Britain. In some cases it was twenty or thirty years before ordained ministers of their denominations came from Britain to minister to them. This first planting of a full Christian community among Africans was a genuine lay movement. Men took their faith with them to their new home and shared it with the recently freed captives landed in their midst from Dahomey, Nigeria, Cameroon and Congo.

Within fifty years of the founding of Freetown, Christian congregations were to be found in many coastal towns in the Gambia, the Gold Coast, Dahomey and Nigeria. They owed their origin to the twin movement of Africans outwards from Freetown and missionaries coming in from Europe, and later from the West Indies and America. Samuel Ajayi Crowther—one of the first six boys to enter the Grammar School of the Church Missionary Society (Anglican) at Fourah Bay, Freetown in 1827 and later Bishop on the Niger—was an example of the former; Thomas Birch Freeman—the Methodist, who visited Kumasi in 1839, Abeokuta in 1842 and Abomey in 1843—of the latter. The somewhat similar founding in 1822 of a home for freed slaves in Liberia under American initiative led to the establishment there of Churches which were likewise a reflection of the religious allegiance of the settlers, this time including Roman Catholics. Monrovia, however, did not form the same springboard for the extension of the Christian faith along the West Coast, since it lacked the kind of harbour that made Freetown the natural link with other trading posts along the West Coast.* It was usually one of these trading posts which became the starting point of local Christian outreach. Missionaries were often led to make one town rather than another their centre through the urging of some ship's captain, himself a member of their Church back home. This was why the Presbyterian Hope Waddell sailed to Calabar from Liverpool and the Methodist Joseph Dunwell to Cape Coast from Bristol.

The European arm of this missionary movement, whether from the Basle Mission, the Church Missionary Society with its many continental missionaries, or the Wesleyan Methodist Missionary Society, was a costly business. In the first twelve years of its work from 1828 at Christiansborg, Accra, the Basle Mission lost eight out of nine men from fever. The cms lost fifty-three men and women in Sierra Leone between 1804 and 1824. The Methodists in the fifteen years following 1835 had seventy-eight new appointments, men and wives, in the Gambia, Sierra Leone and the Gold Coast; thirty of these died within a year of arrival. When the Roman Catholic Society of African Missions began its work in 1859, Bishop de Bresillac, its founder, and the three priests and one lay brother who made up his party, died of yellow fever in Freetown within a few months of arriving. During the following twenty years, one priest of the Society of African Missions died each year—or one in every

* It was, however, from Liberia that in 1914 a travelling evangelist, William Wadé Harris, went preaching through the southern Ivory Coast and brought more men and women to the Christian faith than any single preacher in the history of the Church in Africa.

four of the staff. Marked or unmarked, the graves of these men and women are a factor in the fellowship of African Churches with those in Europe even today, and one which the historian cannot overlook. For the Protestants, this heavy casualty rate meant that for much of the second half of the nineteenth century no more than a holding operation could be maintained, so far as the sending of missionaries was concerned. China and India had wide open doors by 1850 and were making their demands on missionary society resources. Confrontation there with Buddhist and Hindu philosophy called for those who could enter into an understanding of their sacred writings. It is no reflection on the reduced number of men who now served in Africa that, in the main, those with an A.1 life at Lloyd's went to Africa and those with a first at Oxford or Cambridge to the East. This, with the sadly intermittent service of those whose lives were foreshortened, in part accounts for the gaps in the understanding of African religion, culture and language which come under such strong criticism today.

A more positive aspect of this holding operation was the opening it gave for African leadership in the Church. At the village level, the congregation had always been cared for by the village catechist or lay preacher. Now ordained clergy and laymen assumed more responsibility in the central government of the Church. Samuel Crowther of Nigeria and Charles Knight of Sierra Leone among the ordained, and J. P. Brown and F. C. Grant of Ghana among laymen, are ready instances. Later there was to be a setback to this trend, as Ajayi and Webster point out for Nigeria and Bartels for Ghana.[2] The period of colonial rule, even in non-settler West Africa, coincided by the turn of the century with a swing to greater missionary control. This was due not only to the new mood of imperialism but to at least two other factors: the new emphasis on secondary schools and teacher-training colleges with their requirements for qualified staff from overseas, and a new puritanism in some missionaries

[12]

springing from the holiness doctrines of the Keswick Convention.* 3

In Southern Africa, Protestant beginnings were roughly contemporary with those on the West Coast. Here the pioneers were the German Moravians and the London Missionary Society (supported mainly, though not exclusively, by Congregational churches), soon to be followed by British Methodists, the Paris Evangelical Missionary Society, German Lutherans and American Congregationalists. It was in 1797 that the long connection of the London Missionary Society with South-Central Africa began, at first in Namaqualand, later in Bechuanaland and Rhodesia. The names of Johannes Vanderkemp, Robert Moffatt, John Philip and David Livingstone recall not only preachers of the Gospel but those who spoke up for Africans' rights. Mission stations with central boarding schools were soon strung out across Zulu and Xhosa country. Whereas in West Africa the centre of Christian influence was the 'mission house', in Southern Africa it was more often the 'mission station'. Several missionary families lived there together. There were huts for the mission employees who looked after the waggon-teams and worked on the farm. Maize and vegetables were grown for the whole community including the small primary boarding school or training institution. From these stations in the south a northward movement was consistently maintained, though frequently interrupted by Zulu wars and political differences with Boer farmers. Thus, the first permanent contacts with the peoples north of the Limpopo— Matabele, Barotse, Batonga and Ngoni—were made well in advance of the political occupation of the Rhodesias and Nyasaland. The great brick cathedral of the Presbyterian Church in Blantyre was already being built when the British

* The annual series of interdenominational Protestant meetings held in Keswick, England, for the deepening of the personal religious life of those taking part.

flag was raised at Fort Salisbury in 1890. The rapid growth of the Church in this South-Central region was due not only to the pioneer missionaries from Europe and America but also to the Xhosa and Zulu Christians who accompanied them northward as oxen drivers or potential catechists and who were the effective evangelists of these new areas.

In East Africa, German missionaries in the service of the Church Missionary Society reached Zanzibar in 1844, and then crossed to the mainland through Mombasa. Missionaries of the CMS were in Uganda in 1877, and the first White Fathers (Catholic) arrived there two years later. Within ten years, forty-five young men at the Kabaka's court, Catholics and Protestants, were put to death because they were Christians. So rapid, however, was Christian penetration of the court and among the county chiefs that Christians had become the major political force in the country by the time colonial rule began in 1894.

In Central Africa, the Baptist Missionary Society entered the Congo in 1870, to be followed by the first significant group of independent missionaries, whose support on a faith basis led to the foundation of the Interdenominational societies. One of these, the Livingstone Inland Mission of 1878, later became the Congo Balolo Mission, now the Regions Beyond Missionary Union. The Christian and Missionary Alliance followed in 1884, and the Plymouth Brethren in 1886.

That these missions were able to build up their work during the years in which King Leopold personally ruled the Congo by methods which the missionaries bitterly condemned was due to the clauses governing the Congo Basin accepted by the Berlin Conference of 1884-5. They included the following: 'They [the signatory powers] shall, without distinction of creed or nation, protect and favour all religious, scientific or charitable institutions.'

By this time, Roman Catholic missions had already re-entered Africa and the great century of Rome's missionary activity in the continent had begun. Members of the French Holy Ghost Fathers were in Senegal in 1843, and in Angola and Congo in 1866. The tragic end at Freetown in 1859 to the first party of the Lyons Society of African Missions was to spur that body to continued effort until communities of the Catholic faith were as widely established as the Protestant Churches throughout West Africa. In 1878, Bishop Lavigerie's White Fathers set out from North Africa for Tanganyika and, as we have noted, for Uganda. Almost simultaneously, members of this order penetrated southward into the sub-Saharan regions of West Africa. The Scheutveld Fathers, the Order of the Sacred Heart of Mary, were given responsibility in the Congo by King Leopold in 1888, where they were joined in 1892 by the Society of Jesus. In South Africa, the Oblates of Mary the Immaculate had begun their mission in 1851, and in 1884 the Oblates of St Francis de Sales entered South West Africa. Other societies and orders followed in quick succession.

Their progress has been spectacular. There were nearly 2 million Roman Catholics in these countries by 1900, and about 5 million by 1930. Today the number is about 27 million, served by over fifty different Catholic orders from overseas, these having some 14,000 members. What were the causes of this success, when compared with both the earlier Catholic missions and the main thrust of Protestant missionary work in the first three-quarters of the nineteenth century? They were able to profit from the mistakes of the Protestants and their ability to overcome opposition. Catholic missionary activity restarted at a time when control of tropical diseases was making headway; less overshadowed by the continuous death-toll of the past, it was able to attract a new recruitment from the manpower resources of peasant Europe, its agents being drawn in the main from France, Ireland and Belgium. It was helped in its strategy by the over-all responsibility retained by the

Propaganda Fide without at the same time losing the singleness of direction provided by the individual missionary orders. In contrast to the larger Protestant societies, the responsibility of many of the Catholic orders was limited to Africa and even to a particular region in Africa. This made possible a greater concentration of resources.

With the political partition of Africa following the Berlin Conference, European rule began to provide an umbrella of law and order for missionary activity. A settled government, the telegraph, the railway—all helped; and Ross's work on the mosquito was soon to make its contribution. Schools managed by church or mission, with the goodwill of the colonial administration, were soon to increase rapidly. Thus, the high colonial era following 1885 brought enlarged opportunity to European and North American missions. The debit side of the new political environment was not so clearly recognised. For the first time, missionaries were seen by Africans as members of a ruling group, and then of a ruling race. In South-Central and East Africa, they were among those foreigners who received grants of African land from the new governments. That the land was used for mission stations, schools and hospitals in the service of African people did not remove the resentment men felt as they entered the fenced missions which had been their fathers' grazing ground.

For Protestant and Catholic alike, the colonial era ushered in the period in which their resources were concentrated on schools. The missions had been the first providers of schools; soon they were to initiate study for educational planning that would lead to increased demands on them by governments. In North America, the Mission Boards encouraged the Phelps Stokes Fund to undertake two Commissions on Education in Africa (West and Southern Africa 1921, East Africa 1923). In Britain, Dr J. H. Oldham, acting on behalf of the Conference of British Missionary Societies, was largely responsible for the setting up in 1923 of the Advisory Committee on Education to the Secretary of State for the Colonies.

The first impact of these studies was on teacher-training. Where hitherto the village catechist had during the week gathered a handful of boys (but seldom girls) in the mud or bamboo church for instruction in the three Rs, teachers of primary school-leaving standard trained in the new Church training colleges now strengthened the staff. Classroom buildings in their own right were built alongside the church. The minister or priest for the area continued to be the manager. He kept the school accounts and received the increasing sums allocated from government funds to supplement pupils' fees of a shilling or two shillings a month towards the salaries of the teachers. For many years the local congregation made up the difference, and with the help of the local community erected the necessary buildings. At secondary and teacher-training level, monies came from overseas towards buildings, and missionary teachers provided the core of qualified staff. When the governments of independent Africa met at Addis Ababa in 1961 under the auspices of UNESCO to plan the extension of education so as to ensure universal primary schooling throughout the continent by 1980, the foundations on which they were able confidently to build were the result of missionary endeavour dating back to before the founding of Fourah Bay College in 1827, and culminating in a development over the past forty years so intensive as to represent the outpouring of the very life-blood of the Church. An African minister summed it up at the opening of a new school building in 1939. After the cheers for the Chief, the Government Commissioner and the Director of Education had died away, he stepped forward and called out: 'And now three hearty cheers for the unpaid managers of schools.'

★

Up to the end of the nineteenth century, the Christian mission

[17]

in Africa was composed of the two strands we have been describing: Protestant missionary societies related to the long-established Churches—Lutheran, Reformed, Presbyterian, Anglican, Baptist, Methodist, Congregational—and Roman Catholic missionary orders. From about 1880 two further strands begin to appear: a new group of Protestant societies from America and Europe, and, from within Africa, the African Independent Churches.

The new Protestant group itself subdivides. There are missionary societies related to distinctive, though more recently formed, denominations; and there are those which are interdenominational. Among the former are the Salvation Army, the Seventh Day Adventists, the Plymouth Brethren (Christian Missions to Many Lands) and the Pentecostalists (Assemblies of God). The Interdenominational societies sprang from individual efforts, as with some of the early missionaries to Congo; these missionaries and their supporters were not identified with any one Church or ecclesiastical tradition. Among such societies are: the Regions Beyond Missionary Union, the Africa Inland Mission, the Africa Evangelical Fellowship (formerly South Africa General Mission), the Sudan United Mission, the Sudan Interior Mission and the World-wide Evangelization Crusade. Most of these are not only interdenominational but also international, with supporting committees in Europe, America and Australasia. The Sudan United Mission, for example, has Danish, Norwegian, North American, British, Swiss, French, South African, New Zealand and Australian links.

In the main, the Interdenominational societies are conservative in their theology and their interpretation of the Bible, being generally described as 'conservative evangelicals'; a few of them are rigidly fundamentalist. They are also 'faith' missions in the sense that they seek specific financial support for each enterprise through prayer. In large measure, they have

[18]

provided the 'pioneer' missionaries of the twentieth century. They have leapfrogged over the already established missionary areas, planted by the nineteenth-century pioneers from the historic Churches, and have moved into new country, such as the sub-Saharan belt north of the tropical forest in West Africa. Those with up to sixty years' work behind them have themselves now inaugurated Churches, such as the Association of Evangelical Churches of West Africa (ECWA) set up by the Sudan Interior Mission, the Fellowship of Churches of Christ in the Sudan (TEKAS in its Hausa abbreviation) formed by the Sudan United Mission, and the Africa Inland Church formed by the Africa Inland Mission in Kenya.

A more recent flow of small individual faith groups from North America has been very strong since the end of the Second World War. These have often been composed of teams of two or three supported by a single church congregation in America. They have the advantage of starting with a clean slate, not inheriting older traditions from senior missionaries nor having to serve within a Church structure which has become stereotyped. In practice, they tend to develop a pattern all too like the older paternalism. Consequently, where missionaries of older societies are self-critical about the culture-pattern they have carried with them as the clothing of the Gospel, this new generation of independent missionaries seems to accept complete identification of the Christian way with their own national way of life.

In 1962, figures for North American Protestant missionaries serving overseas, not limited to Africa, showed that 39 per cent (10,452) were from boards directly related to denominations in the main stream of Christian tradition and 61 per cent (16,348) to Interdenominational, Evangelical and Faith missions.

The second of the later strands mentioned above is that of the African Independent Churches. So far, the picture we have shown is of Churches coming into being as the direct or indirect

[19]

result of missionary endeavour from overseas. That is by no means the whole of the story. Most of those Churches were moving by the 1960s towards autonomous status or had already achieved it. Their pattern, in constitution, Church order, liturgy and doctrine, was similar to that of their sending Church in Europe or America. Alongside these autonomous historic Churches, other Christian Churches were coming into being—first in South Africa, then in West and East. Initially called 'Separatist', they are now more generally termed 'Independent'. Their founders, in nearly every case, had been members of one of the older established mission Churches. But in South Africa, the Independent Churches have themselves become fissiparous and most new movements there do not now stem directly from the historic Churches. In 1913, there were 30 Independent Churches in South Africa; by 1948 they had become 800, and by 1960, 2,200.

The reasons for the formation of Independent Churches have been many, but most can be contained in one or other of the following: a revolt against European domination in Church or State; a revolt against the practice of the Churches in regard to polygamy; or a revolt against limitation of spontaneous expression in worship such as drumming, handclapping and dancing or of the application of the Christian faith to healing and the related world of witchcraft. Revolt, however, is not a positive enough conception when considering the whole movement. The response of the Holy Spirit to the questing spirit of man, in a situation where the existing Churches were not helping him to meet his deepest need, was to inspire this man or that woman with the gift of prophecy. Too often the Churches' attitude was purely negative; they followed only the first part of the advice of an early Christian pastor and failed to fulfil the second part: 'But do not trust any and every spirit, my friends: test the spirits to see whether they are from God.'[4]

There is in the hymns of certain South African Independent

Churches a strong recurrence of the themes of such Negro spirituals as *No more auction block for me.* A black Messiah is needed 'because people are tired and need one to lead them to a new promised land out of the bondage of living for a life-time in a world the white man has divided, in neither part of which you are really free to be yourself'.[5] This messianic strain became actualised in the later teaching of Simon Kimbangu of the lower Congo, leading him into trouble with the Belgian authorities and to life imprisonment. Following his death and in the few remaining years before independence, he was for his followers their 'black saviour'.

In those parts of the continent where political freedom was not the issue, independence from European supremacy in the Church, whether experienced consciously in Church government or unconsciously in patterns of the liturgy and theological interpretation, was a dominant motive. Usually independence was nourished by the reading of the Bible. There was a going back to the source of the faith in an endeavour to find what was relevant to a felt need. This promoted obedience to the command to witness found in the Gospels, and spurred missionary endeavour. Thus, in West Africa, the 'Church of the Lord (Aladura)' has spread from Nigeria westwards along the coast and also northwards inside Nigeria. This Church started in 1930 in a general healing revival and now has about 80,000 members in the western provinces of Nigeria alone. Reports from many countries in East, South and West Africa confirm that the Independent Church movement is a rapidly spreading form of Christianity. (For statistics, see Appendix I.)

★

There have been, then, these four strands in the spread of the Christian faith throughout the continent: Roman Catholic, Historic Protestant, 'Faith' Protestant, and Independent. Is it possible to state the size of the Christian community resulting from their mission? Statistics are not readily obtainable; they have to be gathered from many different bodies, with varying usages and degrees of reliability. In some countries, census returns include religious affiliation. There is usually a wide discrepancy between the census figures and those returned by the Churches themselves, the former being the larger. (See Appendix I.) The census figures are the claims of individuals or families, including allegiance claimed by virtue of school attendance, whereas the Churches' figures represent the smaller number of their known recognised members. For some purposes, it is the latter which are valid; but for comparison of the groups of people more likely to be receptive to Animist, Muslim and Christian influences, the former figures are more useful.

It is in this broader sense that we attempt an assessment of the comparative size of the religious communities in sub-Saharan Africa. From the figures at present available, the following very general picture can be given: total population of Africa south of the Sahara 230 million; Animists 115 million; Muslims 55 million; Christians 60 million—27 million Roman Catholics, 23 million Protestants, and 10 million Ethiopian Orthodox. (For some other assessments see Appendix I.)

Whether or not we accept this figure of 60 million for the Christian population, it is evident that the rapid and widespread growth in adherents of the Christian faith throughout Africa in this century has been unparalleled in the twenty centuries of the history of the Church, and is an important factor in recent history. Equally important is the question that remains. Has the movement that came from overseas with such magnetic power spent itself, or is it being so remoulded and replenished within Africa that it will win the allegiance of that half of the rapidly increasing population which is under the age of twenty?

3

The Weakness and Strength of the Church at the Coming of National Independence

AS THE VARIOUS colonial territories stood poised by the mid-'fifties on the brink of independence, the Christian Church would seem at first sight to have been in a strong position. To judge by the numbers of men and women to be seen on village paths on their way to church on Sunday morning, this was a people's movement. The most conservative statistics point to a movement claiming adherents in every country in Africa; in most a significant minority, in some a majority, in the aggregate somewhere near a fifth of the total population. It was a movement still growing in numbers. Yet expansion can take place at the expense of inner integrity; in Professor Roland Oliver's words about East Africa, 'the danger is that under the stress of political and social change organised Christianity may start to disintegrate at the centre while it is still expanding at the circumference'.[1] Ominous signs were showing and deep-cutting criticisms being made which suggested that this might be true throughout the continent. Alongside of the growing numbers joining in Christian worship was the rise and fall, and rise yet again, of worship at this or that local shrine, related to an old or new form of traditional religion. Significantly, such worship was attended by many of those who were already experiencing the strain of the new world of business affairs. Against the contention that the Christian Church in Africa was a people's movement came the strongly voiced criticism that the Church had not been as firmly in the van of the independence movement as it should have been in the light of its claim for justice and respect for the individual.

For its members, the Church is a divinely founded fellowship within which the Holy Spirit acts despite the human frailty of members of the fellowship. There is for them an unknown spiritual dimension in any equation the historian seeks to formulate. This does not exonerate us from the attempt to assess the points of weakness and of strength of the Church as it emerged from the colonial era; on the contrary, it demands the utmost honesty for, as the history of the Church repeatedly shows, judgment has to begin with God's own household.[2]

Weaknesses and strengths can be listed. On the one hand, we find missionary control; dependence on funds from overseas; too great an involvement in formal education; disunity between the denominations; an ordained African ministry inadequate in numbers and training; failure in relation to the problems raised by polygamy; a paucity of African expression in worship and of concern for African thought-forms; lack of conviction in the practice of racial equality. On the other hand, we find widespread support; lay witness and leadership; the provision of the Bible in the mother tongue; the provision of education; care for the sick and needy; the sharing in a worldwide fellowship; the reality of personal experience. As we treat these in this order—first the points of weakness and then the points of strength—we shall find some of them moving between the two sides of the equation. For example, it is not possible to describe inadequacies in the ministry of the Church without at the same time referring to the devotion and character of those who compose it.

MISSIONARY CONTROL

A number of Churches were constitutionally autonomous well before national independence. Years before, outside events had forced the change to autonomy in some significant cases. The First World War, to give an example, cut off the Ewe Church of Togo from its parent Bremen Mission. The Togo Church adopted an independent statute which was not abrogated when later it sought a relationship for the service of missionaries and financial aid with the Paris Evangelical Missionary Society. (The story of the influence in this independence movement of Mrs R. Baeta, wife of a senior Ewe pastor, has still to be written; it is not surprising that her daughter became the first West African woman high court judge.) A similar break during the First World War with the parent links brought independence constitutions to the Presbyterian Church in Ghana and the Lutheran Church in northern Tanzania.

It was not until the late 1940s and the 1950s, however, that further instances occurred. The Anglican province of West Africa was constituted in 1951; the provinces in East and Central Africa followed later. The Anglican province of South Africa is nearly a hundred years older, but this was formed in the context of a 'settler' Church. These provinces are autonomous units in the Anglican communion. They are not constitutionally federated, though the Lambeth Conference of bishops representing the world-wide Anglican communion, through its decisions on the norms of Anglican thought, continues to exercise an influence in doctrine and practice. These decisions are not binding, but non-observance could in certain instances lead to non-recognition in the form of a province's declaring that others were out of communion with it. 'Each province knows that if it mis-uses its liberty, or goes beyond certain limits in the exercise of its independence, it is liable to lose a fellowship which it regards as extremely valuable.'[3]

The Presbyterian and Evangelical Churches of Cameroon achieved their autonomy three years before their country. Methodist Churches were slower, that of Ghana not attaining autonomy until 1961, though *de facto* self-government had been in existence for some time. The concept of the corporate body of Methodist preachers, John Wesley's bequest of a Connexion rather than a Church, proved harder to break down into separate autonomous constitutional units.

The Roman Catholic Church progressed from dioceses under the leadership of vicars apostolic to territorial hierarchies at about the same time as the formation of the Anglican provinces: British West Africa in 1950, South and British East Africa in 1951, and French Africa in 1955. These are all part of the Church of Rome, but with self-government within the limits of order and liturgy set down by the Pope or Council of the Church. The co-ordinating point for these hierarchies, of which several now have African archbishops, is the Papal Delegate for the area. In the Roman Catholic Church, therefore, there is a structural development from the mission area to the fully constituted diocese; this development takes place within an integrated world-wide Church and without any thought of radical independence. As soon as possible, nationals are appointed to bishoprics; there were 61 black Africans present among the 2,500 bishops at the second Vatican Council.

Thus, some Churches were already autonomous in the years immediately preceding political independence; some were on the threshold; in others autonomy was scarcely being considered. Yet these different groupings were not clear-cut. A missionary head of an autonomous Church might reflect fully the thinking of his Synod, or might unconsciously be the medium of the thinking of a missionary society overseas. Likewise, an African head of a Church not yet fully autonomous might act as though his Synod was already autonomous, or be subservient to a mission board. In practice, the degree of dependence on decisions taken in New York, London or Berlin was often in direct ratio to the proportion of the Church's budget received ⟵ from overseas. Comparatively rich Churches in Ghana and Nigeria were accustomed to take decisions locally which poorer Churches in, say, Gambia or Dahomey, felt it necessary to refer for final decision overseas. When the writer moved from a teacher-training college in Ghana to a missionary society headquarters in London, he found the missionary head of the Church in Kenya referring to him decisions on the internal running of a college there that, as principal of the Ghana college, he did not even need to refer to his Church head in Accra. In the Ghana case, the principal was spending local money; in the Kenya case, the money was being requested from Britain— yet at the time both Churches had the same degree of constitutional dependence.

The relative place of missionaries in the life of the Church was changing gradually in the period before the achievement of political independence in Africa. Something depended on constitution, much on the climate of local opinion. Where the ethos of a missionary society separated it at the home end from the central structure of the Church, so that it had a marked corporate life of its own, there was a tendency to maintain a separate entity in the mission area when a Church was constituted from the mission. Certain institutions, schools or hospitals might thus remain a direct responsibility of the mission. Missionaries themselves were thought of as lent from outside, rather than as being integral members of the Church with a place in its constitutional organisation arising from such membership. In this pattern, administration relating to missionaries was often kept separate; thus, there might be a mission treasurer as distinct from a church treasurer. In other patterns of relationship missionaries were fully incorporated. This full incorporation is now the more usual practice.

Much depended on the climate of opinion. Missionaries were

influenced by their contemporaries in government and commerce. There was an overemphasis on bureaucratic competence. There was also the heady wine of exercising leadership earlier than would have happened if one had remained at home. A young missionary of the 1920s might well go to West Africa imbued with the spirit of Indian experience expressed in the title of a Student Christian Movement leaflet: 'Not leaders, but servants and saints.' The current philosophy he met in Church and State, in senior missionary and district commissioner, was: 'We are here to train Africans to take over the reins of government, but it won't happen in our time.' This was partly due to conservatism, partly to the nature of the system. This seemed to demand that more weight be put on ability to keep the in-tray clear than on the steady judgement and accumulated wisdom of an older man.

Where missionaries were in positions of authority, they usually recognised the need they had for the judgement and experience of older African pastors when some difficult pastoral issue was before them, and where the life of the local congregation was inextricably bound up with the social patterns of society. There was less readiness to do so in matters of theological principle or ecclesiastical tradition which might as truly underlie those same problems. In Western terms, no African colleagues had as yet received theological training to a graduate standard. This fact, and a looking over the shoulder to keep in step with the theological thought of the tradition from which the missionary came, inhibited greater readiness to share. As a corollary, truths revealed by the Holy Spirit within the fellowship of the Church in Africa did not reach back to influence the theological thought and the practice of the West as quickly as might otherwise have happened. There are seven Union Theological Colleges in Africa, the oldest of them now twenty-five years old; the member churches of the British Council of Churches are still gingerly feeling their way to starting one in Britain.

A factor which delayed the process of devolution from missionary control in East and, more markedly, in Central and Southern Africa, was the presence of white settlers. Pastors of European congregations, and their lay representatives, increased the number of Europeans in the decision-making committees of the Church. More subtly, in the Church as in the political, social and economic spheres, the pressures of a settler-paternalism set at a higher level the point of risk-taking in letting a man out on his own to make or mar a job. A visitor from West Africa to Rhodesia in the early 1950s met senior African teachers in primary schools, whose titular headmasters were missionaries. Even allowing for the shorter history of post-primary education in Rhodesia, in West Africa these teachers would have been headmasters in their own right. In West Africa, events in the countries themselves pushed European Church leaders, not to accept the idea of African leadership—that was already accepted—but into an accelerated implementation of it; but in East and Central Africa, colleagues from outside had to add their weight in the pushing, even towards the acceptance of the principle in the foreseeable future.

To sum up: excess of missionary control and its exercise for too long into the post-1919 world proved a weakness. It was the major factor in the birth of many of the Independent African Churches. It has caused the historic Churches to mark time in the first few years of the high-speed revolution which accompanies national independence; to mark time while new African Church leaders get the feel of the ropes. This need for the new leaders to learn the ropes of administrative routine has inevitably meant that they have less time to concern themselves at once with the vital issues of the Church's relation to, and contribution within, the national revolution.

This judgement is made from within the Church. There are judgements from outside which indicate that the Church, in fact, gave a lead in handing over authority. Indeed, its apparent weakness at times resulted from the State's calling on the services of those whom the Church had prepared for its own leadership, thus laying upon the Church the reproach of relying on the expatriate administration the State was repudiating. *The Ashanti Pioneer*, in the van of the self-government movement in Ghana in the early 1950s, commented in a leader: 'While we cry ourselves hoarse after self-government and africanisation, the Churches silently but surely are laying solid foundations for these; that is, while we labour and trouble ourselves, africanisation and self-government come smoothly and naturally to the Churches. It is the gift of God.' Roland Oliver, remarking on the difference in stability between political and ecclesiastical systems in the transition from dependence to independence, says: 'If there is a historical explanation for this contrast, it must surely be that the planters of East African Christianity were wiser in their generation than their secular colonialist counterparts in their early willingness to share the positions of leadership with their African successors.'[4] Catherine Hoskyns writes of the Congo: 'By 1959 Africans had been given far higher posts in the Church than they had in business or administration. The Catholic Church had already ordained 600 Congolese priests and one auxiliary bishop and the Protestants an equal number of pastors.'[5] And the great French colonial administrator, Robert Delavignette, makes a similar judgement concerning the Church in French-speaking West Africa.[6]

DEPENDENCE ON FUNDS FROM OUTSIDE AFRICA

An indication has already been given that the old adage is still true, that he who pays the piper calls the tune. There is a brake on any fully autonomous decision of policy when another body has to be asked to bear a major part of the cost. However much mutual trust is developed, however genuine the concern of the giving body to divest itself of this remote control, its responsibility in moral stewardship or in legal trust to the subscribers who contribute the money usually makes it impossible to write a blank cheque. This is the problem of neo-colonialism in the Church; it is a problem of stewardship and fellowship, of learning how to give and how to receive. It calls for deeper understanding and trust on both sides, as words of St Vincent de Paul to his novices suggest: 'It is for your love and that alone that men will pardon you for the bread you give them.'

There is another aspect: the pauperisation in spirit of those who look to outside help, not just for a pump-priming operation, but for the year-in and year-out underwriting of their ordinary budget. Yet if it is uneconomical for a weaving shed to be erected on the Ghanaian industrial site at Tema except with the latest non-manual machinery, it may also be unwise to hold back the latest fifty-shilling textbook from the desk of a theological student. Both loom and book are, in their different degree, beyond the average income level of the country; outside aid is needed for both purposes.

Even in countries where the local pastor is fully supported from local funds, the administrative work of the Church—its central offices and its servicing of the congregations through such full-time specialist appointments as that of a National Youth Worker or a Lay Training Officer—is often financed up to 50 or 80 per cent from overseas. A still higher proportion of the financial support of the full-time officers of a National Christian Council and the essential staff of the All-Africa Conference of Churches comes from outside Africa. This support is freely given. The giving springs from the conviction that in the world-wide Church, as in the world-wide community of nations, resources must be shared. The necessity to question such help only arises when it threatens integrity in decision-making, or saps the will to do everything possible from one's own resources including making contributions, however small, to needs outside one's own country.

TIED TO SCHOOLS

In 1923, the Conference of British Missionary Societies, through the pen of Dr J. H. Oldham, submitted to the United Kingdom government a memorandum on African Education: an action that led directly to the setting up of the Advisory Committee on Education in the Colonies, which in its turn did so much to set the direction of educational policy in British Africa during the following thirty years. At that time there were in British Africa among all recognised schools, primary and secondary, 6,000 mission schools and 100 government schools. The balance was different in French colonial territories, with a higher proportion of government schools. In the Belgian Congo, the proportion was much the same as in British Africa, with the difference that more of the mission schools were Roman Catholic. Thus, from the 1920s, there began a partnership between Church and State whereby missions provided management and staff while government bore an increasingly large share of the cost. At the time of the All-Africa Ministers of Education Conference at Addis Ababa in May 1961, it was estimated that 68 per cent of children at school were in schools which were Church-managed or Church-related, approximately 33 per cent of them Protestant and 35 per cent Roman Catholic.

An enterprise of this magnitude was a heavy tax on the resources of the Churches, both in staff and finance. What had begun in the village church as a bush school with an untrained village catechist teaching a handful of boys to read, write and work sums, with the aid of a cast-off reader from a school in Paris or London and a piece of chalk and the end of a packing-case blackened with charcoal, had become a full school with its own purpose-built classrooms, up-to-date equipment and trained teachers, with fees and government grant to account for. This called for management and supervision from the Church which could only be undertaken by those 'unpaid managers of schools', the ordained clergy—missionary and African.[7] Then followed teacher-training colleges and secondary schools, in most cases residential, with their demands on the service of expatriate missionary staff. The clamour of local Christians and the local community (that deputation of a chief and his elders come seventy miles to the local church manager asking for a teacher for their village, willing to sit around for days for the reply; indeed, not willing to return home unless they could take the teacher himself in their triumphant train) was reinforced through the local representatives on a democratically elected Church Synod. The pressure was there all the time to maintain the teacher-training staff at the expense of the theological college, to erect a new dormitory for the secondary school at the expense of the chapel for the teacher-training college, or for the individual missionary to give his spare time to draw up an arithmetic syllabus at the expense of his language study or his understanding of traditional religious thought.

Manifestly, by its very nature the Church is called to serve and to spend itself in service. There is no question but that the service the peoples of Africa have demanded of the Church in these forty to fifty years has been education. Service is always costly. The question that has to be asked, as other weaknesses of the Church are examined, is whether the price paid has been such as to weaken the Church too much and whether it was right to pay it for that particular end. Let one teacher from overseas who was personally involved in the dilemma speak: 'I like to think that the final judgment on the Church that neglected so much of its evangelism to take a part in this educational expansion will be that it could have done no other. It was God's will that the people should wake up to their need of education and that the Church should help them to open this door, for by helping they have made life more abundant for the children of Ghana.'[8]

[33]

To serve in this way was at the same time to be in a position of privilege. Consider it through the eyes of the Church member. As he looked back on the coming of the Church into his own life, he saw, if his own home had been non-Christian, that it was the decision of his father to send him to the village school which had turned his feet into the Church. He learned to repeat the Lord's Prayer at school; it was understood that enrolment in school also implied attendance in church on Sunday morning. A habit began which for him became a commitment. The spiritual interpretation of life which was his home tradition took on a new shape in the liturgy of the village church, whether it was Lutheran, Baptist, Roman Catholic or Anglican. The influence of one or other of his teachers was associated for him with a Church school. So when it comes to his own offspring, his son or grandson must go to a school bearing the Church's name, not only for a successful leaving certificate, not only for character-training, but that he also may become a Church member. The way to Church membership has come to be seen as lying specifically through the Church school rather than through the Church. It is this man's experience that provides the pressure of public opinion which the Kenya Education Commission of 1964 reports when it says that it finds evidence, even though it cannot always be formally assembled, of the wish on the part of parents in many areas that the school should be 'conducted within the spirit of a particular faith and that religious instruction should be given accordingly'.[9] This is positive. Where it so quickly becomes a weakness is where the Church, through its members, ministers or leaders, can see no way of transmitting the faith to the next generation if the opportunity provided by Church schools is taken away. When this happens, the school is snatched at, not as a service to the community, but as an arm of the Church, and one provided by State funds.

From such a position it is not a far step to the mounting

pressures of local Christian communities for schools of their own denominations, and then the worst forms of competition follow. Put bluntly, in a traditional African religious background the chances are that the adoption of a religious commitment in Standard Six in a Church school will decide the effective or nominal relationship of a boy throughout his life. The recent Ghana census reveals this very strongly. This posed a dilemma in pre-independence days when educational development was already thrusting ahead. There would be two infant schools in a village, one Anglican and the other Roman Catholic; or one Presbyterian and the other Methodist. A junior school was wanted, but planning control was now strong enough to prevent either of the Churches from opening a junior school without the permission of the Area Education Committee. The fear of each Church, not just of the minister but the members, was that if the other Church obtained the junior school, and then the senior school, the school allegiance of the boys at the age of Christian initiation would decide their future Church allegiance irrespective of the Church allegiance of their home. The rivalry resulting from this fear has vitiated educational planning in the past, and has provided the easy excuse for those who were not anxious for any Christian influence to say 'a plague on both your houses'.

One further point needs to be made about the Church's position of privilege in education. It was also a position of power. Examine the membership of Government Education Commissions towards the end of the colonial period and you find that they were nearly always composed in about equal numbers of European government administrators and European missionary educators. And through the working week, behind the scenes, telephone conversations between heads of Churches and Education Department officials were a constant part of the moulding process of educational planning. This held two dangers for the Church. The first was that there was no practical need to educate the Christian community in the issues involved in the Church's responsibility in education, nor in the distinctive contribution in educational thinking which the Church should offer to the nation; for the indirect means of influencing government policy through an instructed public opinion was not required when so much could be achieved on an 'old boy' basis. The second—and this spotlights a weakness to be referred to again later—was that, when the Church often had things to criticise in government policy regarding education, the criticism took place in a European context across the committee table or on the telephone. Criticism through the press or through public meetings was seldom expressed. This helped to strengthen the belief that the Church never criticised the colonial government. There was yet a further danger. 'A bigger danger, which the Synod had seen but had been silent about, was the possibility of the Church becoming so dependent on Government, in the name of co-operation, that it might lose that clarity of perception which was its best gift to the good life of the people.'[10]

DISUNITY

The annual shareholders' meetings in London of the great missionary societies in the early 1800s enjoyed cross-membership from various Churches—Anglican, Congregational, Methodist, Baptist—which shared a common concern for the spread of the Gospel in other countries. Tragic losses through death from malaria and yellow fever in West Africa were a common sorrow and a shared challenge in the call for more volunteers. So it was in Africa itself. On his return to Badagry from the first Christian missionary visit to Abeokuta in 1842, the Methodist Thomas Birch Freeman found the Anglican Henry Townsend just arrived. They shared the Christmas Day service together in Badagry. It was when their converts in town and village built

[36]

their respective churches that the sense of oneness in mission became all too quickly dissipated.

That the missionaries themselves did not foresee this was no doubt due to their concern at the immensity of the task before them, for which there could hardly be too many workers, and to the fact that back home, especially in the growing industrial areas, there likewise seemed room for all, judging by the way the new churches and chapels had their pews full on Sundays. In Africa, it was not so much in doctrine as in liturgy and Church government that the differences were felt. In the course of a short generation, African Christians showed themselves remarkably and creatively receptive to the various modes of worship brought to them by the different denominations. The Anglican Prayer Book, the Reformed Liturgy, the hymns stemming from Luther and Wesley, the forms of Church government that placed greater or less power with minister or elders—these features of Protestant Christianity became an integral and enhancing part of the faith of the respective African congregations. Yet, in sustaining the worship of the faithful, they also divided them from one another. This was all in the Protestant tradition. In the deeper division between Protestants and Roman Catholics, all the emotions of generations of confrontation in Europe were reflected in the missions, and the division in Africa tended to be more or less acute according to the home situation from which missionaries came, whether Ireland or France, Britain or Holland. Yet often at the very beginning there was real fellowship, just as with Freeman and Townsend. The Anglican Philip O'Flaherty wrote from Kampala on Christmas Day 1881 of a White Father, his neighbour: 'Livinhac I love, he and I have long walks, talking of the deep things of God.'

The thrust of education accentuated the differences and turned friendly competition into acute rivalry. The religious allegiance of the next generation could be determined by the

Church association of the day school attended there and then; this was not just Christian allegiance, but denominational allegiance. (Do great European Churches and missionary societies recognise themselves in the names given to Christian congregations in one West African language: Baserefo, Romafo, Weserefo, Sepegyifo?) So the very point of service to the community in the name of Christ, the meeting point which afforded the opportunity of presenting the claims of Christian disciple-ship, became also—indeed, often, exclusively—the opportunity to strengthen one denomination at the expense of another. Many unedifying stories could be told of the competition to gain the right to open schools; though equally, even across the Protestant-Catholic barriers of other years, there are stories of understanding and mutual encouragement.

Disunity, then, all too often meant overt rivalry. To those who reflected on the teaching and spirit of the Lord of the Church, this was a sin against the Holy Spirit; to those who sought at independence to maintain the unity of the nation, it was a stumbling-block to national unity. Anything in the body politic, at national or local level, which placed one group in antagonism to another, was to be deprecated and eliminated. In the same context, Christian statesmen who sought to effect reconciliation among different tribes in the new nation found the Church a broken reed, not the strong support it should have been, through lack of reconciliation within itself.

The picture would not be complete without indicating that, while by-gone European struggles of conscience were reflected in the competition between little power-blocs of, say, Presby-terian elders and Methodist leaders in some African village, there was always greater religious tolerance among African Christians than that usually obtaining among Christians in Europe or America. Protestants would support the Harvest Festival of the Roman Catholics as if it was their own. But the tragedy and weakness of division and disunity were there.

[38]

THE AFRICAN MINISTRY

The respect in which the African minister was held in the community was most widespread and at its highest some thirty to forty years ago. When few administrative jobs were open in government or commerce, when already a handful of boys had received some schooling beyond the primary level, to be called and ordained as a minister of the Gospel gave status in the community and a stipend above the average cash earnings. Those who answered the call did so sincerely; but it was comparatively easy for them, since social and family pressures were on the side of the choice they made. Well before the coming of independence, this position had changed. Generally speaking, by the late 'forties the cream of the secondary schools were already going to the universities, overseas or at home, thence to fill the ever-multiplying posts in public administration open to anyone of ability. The Christian ministry had now become the last profession to be considered. Even if it was thought of and longed after, family pressures had usually become too great; responsibility for the education of younger brothers and sisters, nephews and nieces caused an intolerable strain. That a small number of university men are, in fact, entering the ministry is a tribute to the sense of vocation not only of themselves but of their families. Among all the Protestant Churches in the following countries, the number of ordained African ministers who in 1965 were graduates in theology were: Ghana 40, out of 559; Nigeria 49 : 1,500; Cameroon 17 : 700; Kenya 1 : 377; Uganda 2 : 480. The Roman Catholic Church follows its universal method of secondary education for would-be ordinands in junior seminaries, leading on to post-secondary studies in philosophy and then to theology in the seminaries. Their comparable graduate figures were therefore: Ghana 82; Kenya 66; Uganda 257.

The majority of those who entered the Protestant ministry

had usually served the Church previously as catechists or school teachers. Brought up in village life, accustomed to the pattern of village Church fellowship, they became managers of groups of village schools, dispensers of the sacraments to scattered village congregations, pastors and arbitrators in disputes. Such a minister might then be stationed to the care of a large congregation in a rapidly expanding town. With no sociological training, he attempted to repeat the village pattern on a town scale. For all his pastoral concern, he was unable intellectually to meet the needs of those with the new opportunities for higher education, nor was he able to adapt the pattern of the Church's life to town ways. So, perhaps, he fulminated against the burial and mutual benefit clubs which grew up among his members, failing to recognise in them an unconscious attempt to create something of the smaller community group which their need craved.[11]

This African ministry—in character the salt of the earth, the first echelon of Africans to receive authority and responsibility under European rule—had fallen behind, as so often happens with pioneers. Their integrity had made possible the nation's trust in the Church's management of schools which involved the handling of large sums of public money under a skeleton auditing system. They would be the first to admit that the price which had to be paid for thus serving the schools was the loss of their all-too-scanty time for theological reading—such reading as related biblical insights to the spiritual, psychological, mental and sociological problems of the community whose pastors they were.

In West Africa, and maybe elsewhere, a further weakness of the ministry has been the deep mistrust that has developed between its members and the laity. The clericalism exported from the West, allied to the African concept of the chiefs, has been accentuated by the relatively low educational standard of so many of the ministers. This has placed them on the defensive,

[40]

making them less ready to share their one security: their position of privilege in Church government.

A weakness in the pattern lay at the heart of the attempt to serve the many members in widespread congregations through full-time ministers. Some village congregations never had the sacrament or the mass celebrated in their midst; they had to travel many miles to an occasional central service. Or a minister might arrive in a village late one afternoon and celebrate communion before daybreak the following morning before moving on to his next call; just once or twice in a year, and never on a Sunday. A Catholic writer comments on this weakness: 'More and more it is obvious that Catholic life requires the celebration of the eucharist in every sizeable group of Catholics every Sunday. Our present system of priest formation will never even begin to achieve that, and a eucharist-less Church is a lifeless body.'[12] Similarly, Bishop Bengt Sundkler at the end of *The Christian Ministry in Africa* writes: 'The local church needs its own pastor and priest again to be a "mid-man" fully equipped with all the authority of the Church, administering the Word and the Sacraments in the midst of the village.'[13] In an article in the *African Ecclesiastical Review* of April 1966, Adrian Hastings compares the one priest for 644 Catholics in England with the one for 1,800 in Africa. He calculates that, if the Catholic community and the number of priests in Africa grow at their present rate, this ratio will have become one in 3,500 by the year 2000: an estimate which is, in fact, already approached in Uganda, where the figure is one in 3,333. It is evident that in both Catholic and Protestant Churches a new pattern of the ministry is urgently needed.

POLYGAMY

At no point has the Christian message and ethic broken more radically into the life of Africa than in the demand on the

[41]

family structure that it should accept monogamy as the marriage pattern for those of its members who become Christian. This has resulted in open conflict with the family and community, and given rise to secret conflict in the mind and life of many Christians. The ruling of the first missionaries was almost universally that polygynous men should at their conversion to the Christian faith put away all but one wife; otherwise they could not receive the sacraments of baptism and holy communion. There were some who did not think it right to break the existing marriage relationships, and who therefore sought to retain such a man within the fellowship of Sunday worship and Bible study, but withheld the sacraments, though doing so with a feeling that the Church's practice was at odds with the spirit of its Lord. The practice regarding wives varied. Usually they were allowed to become communicant members if the marriage had taken place before conversion. For a man or woman who entered into a polygamous marriage after becoming a member, the discipline of the Church was exercised, and so long as a polygamous state lasted attendance at communion was forbidden.

This strict rule did not carry the conviction of all who became Christians. There have been all too many cases of prominent Church leaders who have taken a second wife secretly—a fact known to the community and kept from the minister, or seen by him with a blind eye. So, when a humbler member suffered the full discipline of the Church, the integrity of the Church was put in hazard—as it was when, with polygamy under discipline, a falling-short of the Christian ideal in temper or covetousness went without pastoral rebuke.

There were two sides to the weakness of the Church's position: its Christian witness failed to understand fully and to provide for the social implications of its teaching; and it was vulnerable to criticism about the operation of its discipline. The dilemma the Church faced was no easy one. How to hold up a new standard before a whole community and yet allow into the fellowship those who were not able to follow it? Many ministers today, African and missionary, if they were starting *de novo* would have the Church grant full communicant status to first-generation Christians who were polygynous. Not all African women would agree. They would say that the very difficulties encountered by the Church show how hard it is to achieve acceptance of the equal personality of men and women, and that they owe to the Church's policy all that has so far been won. Words of Dr Kenneth Kirk are applicable to this, the African Church's greatest single problem:

> The Church must always and everywhere set before men the highest standard she knows in conduct, the truest forms of worship and creed. But she must be very slow indeed to enforce them even by the threat of confining her membership to those who acquiesce. The shepherd's staff and not the tyrant's sword must be her true weapon. The whole flock is to be led into the fold, not the few harried into it whilst the many are left to their fate.[14]

Too often, the insistence on monogamy has led, not to the full enrichment of personality in a one-and-one relationship of mutual love and respect, but to a marriage which is merely not-polygamy. Throughout Africa today, there are those seeking, both in study groups and within their own family life, a Christian view of personality and social life which finds its fullest expression in monogamy and which can replace the natural man's view of personality and social life which finds expression in polygamy in Africa and in successive marriages in *good point* Europe and America. Some have already found this; alongside the instances of Christian polygamy given in his recent book on the Togo Church, Debrunner comments on the number of successful monogamous Christian marriages that have stood the test of time in a Togo village.[15]

[43]

RACE RELATIONS

At the heart of the teaching of Jesus of Nazareth was an all-embracing love that had no time for distinctions of class or nation. He narrowly escaped death in Nazareth itself when he reminded the worshippers in the synagogue there that, in two outstanding incidents in their people's history, a prophet had been more engaged in helping foreigners than Jews. Twice he broke through the confines of Judaic nationalism in the direction of Samaria, speaking of a worship that superseded that of the Temple in Jerusalem and of a compassion that transcended national barriers. The Church broke out into the Roman Empire only because the Apostle Paul was willing to set aside precious national religious traditions in order that he might be true to the spirit of his Master. It is this faith and this Church which have been brought to the peoples of Africa by white missionaries. They, like Paul, have had to struggle to break through that which in their own inheritance was not of the essence of the Gospel. They have by no means always succeeded. The local patriotisms which help to teach children the meaning of loyalty tend, after the lesson is learned, to go on to demand that loyalty at the expense of foreign groups. A British missionary was inclined to give a British political officer the benefit of the doubt when his word conflicted with an African's. It was easier for an American missionary to criticise the government in a Portuguese colony, an English missionary that in a Belgian, a French missionary that in a British. The conflict of loyalties was intensified where there were large settler communities receiving the ministrations of the Church.

A weakness of the Church in African eyes has been the resultant lack of conviction in the practice of racial equality. This is seen by them most starkly in South Africa, but as definitely in many other countries. The gravamen of the charge is not only the unwillingness of Europeans to worship together

[44]

with Africans—or, when inter-racial worship is practised, the unwillingness to extend this fellowship to social life; it reaches back to the unwillingness to recognise the handicaps involved in segregation in housing, schools, amenities—or, if these are recognised, the unwillingness to press hard in the political field for segregation to be abolished. And, behind all, lies the implied inferiority of a whole people.

The issue of cultural standards is complex. Who is to judge when the point is reached that standards of culture are imperilled? And what is the relation of this to the fellowship of the Church? Europeans are more germ-conscious in this generation than ever before. Missionaries have avoided the hospitality of African homes because of the fear that the drinking water was not boiled. It almost seems as if a man's adulthood and right to vote are to be judged by his knowledge of the working of a flush toilet. Shakespeare and Milton are nearer to African village life than are today's Londoners.

To this charge of racial superiority there have been well-known, and many more unknown, exceptions among European Christians. Yet they only serve to spotlight the grave failure of the Christian witness at this point: a failure which, though critical in our day, does not stand alone. It has its parallel within the Church in the class divisions of Western society and in the contempt with which the Akan have viewed the Dagarti or Moshi, with which the Creole in Sierra Leone and Liberia have viewed the indigenous peoples there.

AN AFRICAN EXPRESSION OF THE CHRISTIAN FAITH

We come to the last, and what many African Christians now regard as the most crucial, of the points of weakness of the Church: its slowness in becoming an African Church in worship and theological understanding. There are those in the universal Church who would deny, on theological grounds, that there

[45]

can be such a concept as a 'European Christianity' or an 'African Christianity', a 'European' or 'African' theology, a 'European' or 'African' liturgy. The Christian faith, it is argued, in its essence and in its expression must transcend human differences. In this debate, a European writer can all too easily give the impression that he is making the kind of distinction between European and African which is, in effect, a comparison of two cultures to the disadvantage of one of them.[16]

At the heart of the Christian faith lies the statement, 'The Word became flesh'.[17] The two notions of 'Word' and 'flesh' have to be held together in tension. The faith delivered to the saints is an eternal Word of God, unchangeable. The manifestation of that Word was in the flesh of a man of the Jewish people in the first century AD. There can then be only one theology, understood more clearly as succeeding generations of Christians from different backgrounds bring to its study light shed through their own experience by the spirit of truth. Yet the Word becomes incarnate for each generation, and if it is in every generation to be 'touched and handled' so as to be universally recognised, it must be incarnate in the language and life of every people.[18] In this sense, there is need for an African liturgy and an African theology. In this sense, then, the Church has been slow to become African. A report of the Church in Nigeria speaking of the forms of worship of Independent Churches says: 'They make an appeal to African emotions that sometimes makes the most ardent and loyal Churchmen linger round their places of worship with a sincere longing to join in the service in which expression is being given to the inner urge of the worshipper.'[19]

Our European and African cultures have impinged on one another, and for some two or three generations the European has been dominant. As you travelled in Africa you knew you were in a British colony by the 9-hole golfcourse just beyond the European residential area. A French colony proclaimed itself

[46]

by the baguettes on sale in time for petit déjeuner. Or, more simply, you drove on the left or on the right. Similarly, the tower of a village church spoke of a German-Swiss missionary inheritance, a rectangular unadorned chapel of a British Methodist origin. Inside, translated into a local tongue, though robbed in part of its natural rhythm, were hymns set to a German chorale, a pre-Reformation plainsong, an *Ancient and Modern* tune or a hymn of Moody and Sankey whose memorised refrain was spiritual food to the illiterate. Rarely was there a matching of the great liturgical traditions of the Church with the full rhythm and colour of African life. There were, it is true, the moving traditional tunes of the Xhosa and Zulu hymnbooks, and the Fante lyrics; the moments in processions when the swaying of the body gave expression to deep feelings of joy; the uninhibited waving of the leaves of the oil-palm by educated and non-schooled alike during the Palm Sunday hymns; the wood-carving and painting from Roman Catholic Awka and Anglo-Catholic Cyrene; and moments of revelation in miming and dramatisation. One European's understanding of the parables is heightened by the picture of the Ivory Coast man, changed into his best cloth and eager to respond to the invitation to the great feast, who, as he stepped out, felt the restraining hand on his shoulder of the determined-looking woman he had just married. More movingly, his understanding of the Passion is deepened by the memory of a man stumbling under the weight of a heavy baulk of timber up the aisle of the great Anglican cathedral at Kampala. But, in general, the Churches of Africa are still waiting for their own poets, musicians and dramatists to express in African accents the record of their Lord's earthly life, the story of the salvation He has wrought, and the experience of those in whose daily life the Holy Spirit is revealed.

This problem goes below expression to understanding. The mission was planted before the period of scientific anthropological study. There were no sacred books to afford a mine for understanding the religious thought of the people to whom the missionary came. Too often, as on the West Coast, the length of service of individuals was counted in months rather than years. They passed on the message of salvation through whatever medium was available, with too little opportunity to stop and listen to what was already there. The picture in their minds from before leaving their home was of a debased paganism, with ritual human sacrifice standing out most starkly. Lack of understanding undoubtedly exaggerated the evil in customary rites. What some of the missionaries saw, and what their first converts knew, has to be weighed by those who today go to the other swing of the pendulum. The words of W. M. Macmillan are worth recalling: 'The early missionaries called [African rites] heathen superstitions, and themselves having more faith they were perhaps better judges than we are.'[20] And Dr C. G. Baeta, in his contribution to *Christianity and African Culture*, says:

It is idle now to wonder what would have happened if the other line of approach, that of adaptation and fusion, had been adopted. The now common assumption that thereby success would have been guaranteed appears to me to be an unwarrantedly large one. My personal view is that the true character of Christianity would have been completely blurred whereas now, even if it has not flourished among us as we would have liked, at least we know what it is like.[21]

★

Even so, the case is clearly made out for the judgement that the Church has come inadequately to grips with the African thought-world. Dr K. A. Busia, speaking on the occasion of the silver jubilee of the Christian Council of Ghana in November 1954, said: 'For conversion to the Christian faith to be more than

[48]

superficial, the Christian Church must come to grips with traditional beliefs and practices, and with the world-view that those beliefs and practices imply.'[22] He emphasised particularly the concept of group life as distinct from the individualistic concept. It was to take up the challenge of these words that the Christian Council Consultation on Christianity and African Culture was held the following year.

There were unexpressed depths of African experience that were never fully known; therefore the conscious preaching of the Gospel never fully met man there. A missionary preacher in a village church becomes aware that something he has said as he expounds a Bible passage or, more significantly, that he has read in a passage that seems to him to have no immediate relevance, stirs a sudden and deep response from his congregation. Only a life-time of putting such moments of insight together brings the beginning of an understanding of the deeply felt needs of men and women. African pastors and theologians, set free from mental dependence on missionaries and using the methods of pastoral psychology and mental healing, will come more quickly to the diagnosis of those needs and the prescription for their answer. For example, Dr M. J. Field shows in her case histories at one of the traditional shrines in northern Ashanti the cathartic value of public confession.[23] Yet in the Churches of the area, neither the private confession to the Catholic priest nor the spoken testimony to the group in the Methodist class-meeting had been adapted to meet that need. Perhaps the weekly meetings of the Balokole, the Christians of the East African Revival, come near to fulfilling it.* It is of educated members of an East African Independent Church (the African Israel Church Ninevah) that Welbourn and Ogot write: 'Here are men who have found, through the purifying experience of

---

* This revival began about 1935 in Rwanda and Uganda, and it quickly spread to Kenya and Tanzania. (See Taylor, *The Growth of the Church in Buganda*, pp. 99–104.)

5--CATNA

public confession and the ecstasy of "receiving the Spirit", a faith which inspires them to more effective relationship with their neighbours.'[24] Yet such essays by the Church still remain exceptional.

Dr S. G. Williamson has summed up the factual situation at the close of his *Akan Religion and the Christian Faith*: 'The conviction that the Christian faith and Akan religion, encountering each other out of vastly different backgrounds and experience, view each other from a distance without common ground of fellowship, so that the impact never amounts to a real encounter, cannot be set aside.'[25] To which judgement, other words of Dr Busia suggest the response on the part of the Church: 'The new convert is poised between two worlds: the old traditions and customs he is striving to leave behind, the new beliefs and practices to which he is still a stranger. The Church would help him better, if she understood the former while she spoke with authority about the latter.'[26]

★

Any attempt to assess the position of the Christian Church in Africa in the next decade must take full account of these and other points of weakness in its life and witness. What can be put on the other side of the balance sheet? In what lies the strength of a movement which has some 60 million adherents in Africa south of the Sahara?

THE WIDESPREAD NATURE OF THE CHURCH

The very numbers of African Christians indicate that this is not a movement restricted to the elite, whether the tiny elite of university graduates and national leaders, or the wider elite of the schooled. It is a movement of the people. It comprises peasant men and women returning home in the late afternoon from their farms along forest or veldt paths with a Christian hymn as their walking song. They are typified by the red blouses of the Southern African women's movement to be seen every Thursday afternoon in town and village; typified individually in the simple decision of a non-schooled woman in Kenya, only a few years old in the Christian faith, who died rather than take the Mau-Mau oath—doing so, not because she was unaware of land grievances, but because she could not drink the cup of the oath at the same time as the cup of her Saviour's communion. Wherever there is a group of worshippers, they have built a church, if only of palm branches or rough mud. If you were to set out to walk from Freetown across Sierra Leone, Guinea, Liberia, the Ivory Coast, Ghana, Togo, Dahomey to Calabar in Nigeria, and then on through Yaoundé, Kinshasa, Lubumbashi and Lusaka to Salisbury; and if at the end of each day's fifteen miles you came to a village, the odds would be on your being able to say your prayers in a church every night.

Nor is this only a village movement. It is not surprising, and could be predicted, that many youngsters who pass through Church schools and drift to the towns do not retain a vital allegiance to the Church. What is surprising, and this happens time and again, is to meet such a youngster—now head of a family and holding down an important post in the community —worshipping on Sunday morning and applying his faith to his daily job. The membership of the Church covers the widest spectrum, rich and poor, illiterate and literate, cabinet minister and ambassador, trader and overseas merchant, lorry-driver and mechanical engineer, verandah boy and society lady.

Not only is the Church widespread; it now goes back for more than one generation. The experience of a European, after conducting evening worship in a village near the Ghana coast in 1948, of being told by an old leader that it must be sixty years since a European had preached in their pulpit, could be matched elsewhere. A pastor who died in Anecho in 1961 at the age of ninety-nine had been baptised into the Christian faith as an infant; his great-nephew, himself a pastor, is Assistant Secretary of the All-Africa Conference of Churches. The church bell is a sound old people throughout Africa associate with childhood memories, whether it be the clear ring of a foundry-cast bell or the harsher note changing with the years as a strung-up axe-head has given way to a length of railway line, giving way in its turn to the rim of a lorry wheel.

LAY WITNESS AND LEADERSHIP

Because this has been a people's movement, out of it has evolved lay leadership, whether encouraged by the constitution of a democratically governed Church or by the force of circumstances in the more clerically governed Churches. The multitude of village congregations and the scarcity of ordained ministers compelled the recognition of lay leadership. A by-product has been experience in democratic decision-making by local leaders and elders. In the interval between the old tribal council decisions and those of more recently elected local and regional councils—a period covering the era of colonial rule during which administrators and their technical advisers made the decisions in secular affairs—presbyteries and synods discussed the affairs of the Church. In areas where settlers dominated government, this was a valuable safety-valve; the Church was often the only element in African life in which Africans were free to discuss, to reach compromise, to reflect common agreement.

More important, it was through lay men and women much more than through the ordained clergy, whether missionaries or Africans, that the Church grew. The coast trader thrusting up-country into new villages, or the junior government officer transferred to a clerkship in the District Commissioner's office or as dresser in the hospital: such a man gathered others round him on Sunday morning for worship; and the Church grew. Ask for the story of the beginning of the Church in a village or small town anywhere in Africa and the chances are you will be told, not how missionary X or African pastor Y came and preached in the village street, but how trader A—man or woman from a strange town—or schoolboy B, who went from the village seeking schooling and came back a Church member, asked the chief to allot a piece of land for the erection of a bamboo or mud chapel, and with the aid of a few men erected it. Your informant probably adds something like this: 'It was the year after the influenza (i.e., 1919). I was there with my cutlass and helped to cut the line through the bush that the chief pointed out; the land for the Church goes as far as that silk cotton tree and then across to that ant-hill. My father gave twelve shillings. It cost us £30; we paid the sawyers £8 and the carpenter £6; we sent messengers with £16; they brought back 12 packets of nails costing two shillings each, three bundles of iron sheets costing £4 10s. each and some door-handles and hinges.' (When will New Testament commentators learn how retentive of detail the memory is in a pre-literate society?) This lay missionary movement did not, however, always cross major cultural barriers, as from the Creole to the Temne and the Mende, or the Akan to the Dagomba.

In old faded lists of Church members and leaders, the names of women are as numerous as those of men. Among those who first bore witness to the new faith, among those who became leaders of the local Church, among those who gave their labour in building chapel or school or catechist's house, were young mothers as well as old grandmothers. With all our recognition that large areas of experience related to birth and death remained unchanged by the new faith, we have to accept that, as a woman prayed in church, she showed that the name of Jesus had begun to touch those depths; she took part in witness and leader-ship because of a reality that was an intimate part of her being.

[53]

This deep involvement of the common people may well outlive the memory of excessive missionary oversight and control.
A more recent aspect of the strength of lay leadership is seen
in the obverse of the weakness of the ordained ministry—in
theological study. Several African universities have departments of Religious Studies: Fourah Bay, Legon, Ibadan,
Nsukka, Makerere, Salisbury. As we have noted, the number
of future ministers qualified to undergo a graduate course in
theology has been very small. These departments have been
able to maintain staff and justify this against the demands of
the sciences because, in a three-subject Arts degree, there has
been a steady flow of men and women offering theology as one
of their subjects. Their intention has usually been to teach
Religious Knowledge in secondary school or teacher-training
college. This means that in Ghana, Sierra Leone and Nigeria
there are now more laymen in the pew with theology as one
subject of a degree than there are ministers in the pulpit with
a B.D.

THE BIBLE IN THE MOTHER TONGUE

When the first complete Bible in the Asante dialect of Twi-Akan
was welcomed in a public service in 1965, a thousand copies
were sold within an hour. The demand was so great that
traders who had any stocks left were selling out at double the
published price. There are now 77 African languages with the
complete Bible, 116 with the New Testament only, and 220
with only part, usually one of the Gospels. Of these 413 trans-
lations, one was made before the founding of the British and
Foreign Bible Society in 1804, 21 between then and 1850, 94
from 1850 to 1900, and 293 since 1900. Amid so much that was
breaking up traditional life, especially Western education in a
metropolitan language, the Bible was often the one book available in the mother tongue. This was frequently followed by

Bunyan's *Pilgrim's Progress*, now available in 56 African languages.*

The urge to translate the Bible into every language may have helped to prolong the life of a dialect where reason suggested it ought to lose itself in a regional *lingua franca*. There are always two views on this question. What is important is that men and women, not least women, without any schooling on the Western pattern, learned to read in their own language because the Bible was there. In the days before special adult literacy programmes inspired by Dr Laubach's methods, an old grandmother would come to Sunday School week after week painfully learning the alphabet, then short words, then sentences. Then came the day when, with a friend finding the place for her in the Bible bought at the market that week with her saved-up shillings, her face shone with the joy of recognising, as she read, treasured words learned by heart long ago—a sentence from the 14th chapter of John's Gospel or the story of the woman sweeping her room for a lost coin.

The Bible strengthened the Church among the people. It was a family business, the reading of the Word, as anyone knows who has been privileged to come out of the guestroom into the hall of a compound house as the sounds of dawn strengthen and by the light of an oil lamp share in the Bible-reading and the family prayer.

The process of translation helped to heal the divisions of the Church. Representatives of all the Churches in the language area shared in the translation work; that is, the Protestant Churches. 'What has brought Protestant missions together more than anything else has been fellowship in the work of the translation of the Bible.' What is said of the British and Foreign

* Complementary to this was the general encouragement of Christian literature, particularly in the quarterly *Books for Africa*, initiated in 1931 by Miss Margaret Wrong of the International Committee on Christian Literature for Africa: a periodical that ran for thirty years.

Bible Society is true of all the Bible Societies: 'From its inception in 1804 the British and Foreign Bible Society was ecumenical in constitution, in outlook, and in purpose.'[27] Active co-operation in translation is also now taking place between Protestants and Catholics. Protestant versions in a number of languages have been used through the years by Catholic missions.

The patient work of translation has also helped in the study of African religion. As little groups of two or three have wrestled to find the best word to translate some New Testament concept, they have come more closely to grips with African religious thought than in their previous preaching.

THE PROVISION OF EDUCATION

Many of the younger generation retain, amid much criticism, affection for the Church, because it is seen to have answered the felt need of their people for education. The infants' classes in the village church, through the standards' classes in the village school proper, have led to one or other of the Church secondary schools whose names once spelled the only higher education in the country, and which still hold an honoured place within today's greatly increased opportunities. The very history of the independence movement can be spelled out across the continent by the names of Church schools: Annie Walshs Girls' School at Freetown, Sierra Leone; the College of West Africa, Monrovia, Liberia; St Augustine's, Mfantsipim, Wesley Girls' High School and Adisadel—all in Cape Coast, Ghana; in Nigeria, the Baptist Academy and St Gregory's at Lagos, St Anne's, Ibadan, Dennis Memorial, Onitsha, and Hope Waddell, Calabar; Kimpesi College in the Congo; King's School, Budo, and St Joseph's, Masaka, in Uganda; Alliance High School, Kikuyu, Kenya; St Francis and Ashira in Tanzania; Tegwani and Hope Fountain in Rhodesia; Mapanza in Zambia and, in South Africa, Marianhill, Tiger Kloof, Adams, Lovedale,

Healdtown and St Martin's. (The last five, following the Bantu Education Act, are no longer Church foundations.) The relation of such schools to independence is well illustrated by the case of the Alliance High School in Kenya, former pupils of which provided more than half of Mr Jomo Kenyatta's first government. Nor should the contribution of many celebrated teacher-training colleges be overlooked. Not only did they produce teachers but, in the absence of widespread secondary-school opportunities, they provided higher education for many who were destined to serve in other spheres than teaching.

It was not only that the key to a job in the Western-organised economy was provided by these schools. In debates in Church councils, or in words spoken with conviction by leading citizens on speech days, the emphasis is as much on character-training as on academic success. An experienced administrator, speaking at one such speech day, referred to old boys of the school whom he had met at close quarters in his years of service in the country, and described the quality he found in them as 'compounded of mental discipline, mental honesty and moral courage'.[28] This is today a source of resistance to graft and corruption in the public services. An old student of a Church teacher-training college, now a permanent under-secretary in the government of his independent country, could say in a message of greeting to a former vice-principal of the college: 'We are able to do what we are doing in our country's administration today because we saw that the standards you expected of us in college you first expected of yourself.' For many, integrity of Christian living was first seen, not in pulpit preaching, but in the character and conduct of the teacher in the classroom and the housemaster in the dormitory.

CARE FOR THE SICK AND NEEDY

Not long in time after the opening of schools came the provision by missionaries of hospital and medical care. As the only Europeans in their area, most missionaries were unqualified dressers, having a three- or six-month course in first-aid and tropical medicine. Much was done by way of example and with a medicine chest containing epsom salts, quinine, aspirin, acriflavine, boracic and iodoform powders, and lysol. What was done in this way brought home poignantly how much more could be done by a qualified doctor or midwife. So a doctor and a nurse arrived to assist the evangelist and school teacher. A two-ward hospital with a simple operating room was built. The nurse began to train local boys and girls as dressers. Standards of cleanliness and patterns of loving care for the sick and disabled were seen in the mission hospital. Trust sometimes came only slowly. It was a red-letter day when a woman undergoing a difficult confinement was persuaded to come into hospital; no wonder a special prayer was said for God's blessing on the doctor's skill and nurse's care, for on them that day depended the future confidence of the mothers and grand-mothers of the neighbourhood. Confidence by the community in Christian healing often sprang from their marvelling that a single woman from America or Europe was prepared to make her home alone in some distant bush village.

Then the development came. A cluster of out-station dispensaries related to the central hospital were staffed by nurses trained in the hospital. Training progressed from dressers to midwives, to certificated nurses and dispensers. Midwifery led to child care, to research into the nutritional deficiency causes of children's stunted growth, and to baby homes where those whose mothers died in childbirth could be cared for until, after weaning, the family could take them back. Settlement villages for leprosy patients, where they could spend the rest of their lives with what amelioration was possible for their dismember-ment and helplessness, gave way with the discovery of modern drugs to out-patient treatment and rehabilitation centres. The loving devotion of the successors in Africa of Father Damien not only brought happiness to many who were never cured, but itself inspired research and was the patient handmaid of the laboratory scientists in perfecting new treatment.

There were those in government service—some Christian, some not—who gave their service with as great devotion and care. It was, however, more often the small mission hospital with its conscious and declared centre in the small room set aside for hospital prayers which broke into the deep-seated resistance of tradition when the fear of sickness seized a whole family. Thanks came to be rendered for this service not only to the hospital staff but to the God they worshipped. As Dr Z. K. Matthews, of Fort Hare and Geneva, has written: 'The Church has always been most vital when it has ministered to the whole of man. . . . It has done this in varying degrees in the history of its mission in Africa, and it is for this reason that it is so firmly rooted in some parts of the continent.'[29]

A WORLD-WIDE FELLOWSHIP

A further point of strength is seen in the world fellowship of which the local Church was a part. If missionaries embodied what seems at first sight only a one-way flow from Europe and America to Africa, there was developing a sense of oneness with the Church throughout the world. An early example of two-way traffic is quoted from Nigeria by Dr J. F. A. Ajayi.[30] It closely reflects the New Testament experience when Churches in Macedonia sent gifts to meet the need of Christians in Jerusalem, both in regard to the material gifts themselves and the fellowship they embodied. In 1867, Lancashire was hit by a severe depression due to the impact of the American Civil War on the cotton trade. A 'Lancashire Relief Fund' was set up within British Methodism; it received a gift of £10 7s. from the Methodist Church in Abeokuta, just twenty-five years after

[59]

the first preaching of the Gospel there by Freeman. A somewhat similar 'solidarity' in the reverse direction was experienced by a missionary from Ashanti in the winter of 1937. He was speaking at the annual missionary meeting in a small Lancashire village. Its one cotton mill specialised in weaving designs which appealed to the fashion tastes of Ashanti women. Ashanti farmers were holding back their cocoa from sale in the demand for higher prices; their wives had no money to buy new cloths; current stocks were piled high in the Kumasi stores. The order books for the following season of the Lancashire mill were empty; almost the whole village was out of work. There was a record collection, for the Church in Ashanti.

In such practical ways, as well as in prayer and world-wide conferences, there is mutual strength and a deepening of fellowship.

PERSONAL EXPERIENCE

Even a casual contact with the Christian Church in Africa provides glimpses into spiritual experience which is real and vital. The careful and sympathetic analysis by S. G. Williamson in *Akan Religion and the Christian Faith* seems to minimise this in one important particular. He speaks on the one hand of the majority of converts who regard the Christian as 'one who does not go to fetish, attends church, and pays his dues, and is obedient to Church rules'; he describes this approach as largely negative, in times of personal crisis leading to a relapse into traditional practices. On the other hand, he says that 'the limited few, by means of a long process of "europeanization" have learned to assimilate and express, in faith and conduct, the missionary's brand of Christianity'.[31] Every word Williamson uses has to be taken seriously, but this is too hard and fast a line to draw. There are many who, when questioned, would give the answer which seems to place them squarely in the first category, but who, 'in faith and conduct', show that the springs of their being are already deeply affected through the worship and fellowship of the Christian congregation to which they belong.

The dimension which has to be given adequate weight in the summing up is the commerce of God with each individual soul. He takes each one just where that one is: at a traditional shrine or in a cathedral or in a village church halfway between these. The worshipper in the village church repeats the Apostles' Creed and sings 'How sweet the Name of Jesus sounds in a believer's ear, It soothes his sorrow, heals his wounds and drives away his fear'—in conjunction with what the observer cannot but assume are unresolved conscious or subconscious fears of the lesser elements in the spiritual world. In this he has a valid experience of God from which other believers dare not withhold the name 'Christian'. Is not the same mixture of motives and experiences reflected in the first Christian letters, and down the ages since then? May they not be equally so in the refined intellectuality of much European Christianity? Dr Max Warren has a word about the 'younger Churches' in his *Missionary Movement from Britain*: 'They are young only in the duration of their local institutional life. They share with us, neither less nor more, in the whole length of Christian experience from the first day until now. Nor does the Holy Spirit need our mediation by virtue of our greater endowment with His gifts.'[32] Many a Western Christian has been rebuked by the spiritual insight and devotion to Christ of those who have not had a long period of exposure to 'europeanisation', whether they be illiterate villagers or educated townsmen.

Dr C. G. Baeta comes near to this when he says:

I very much doubt the quite generally held view that Christianity has not struck very deep roots here. Again and again, especially in my dealings with groups of Christians such as local congregations or Church conferences and synods, I have been amazed to see how people who had set themselves with great determination upon a course along which they hoped to gain some parochial advantage, when challenged with a word of Scripture or some other reminder of their Christian profession, would often quite suddenly turn round and abandon their ambition in answer to the Christian call, even though it be contrary to their interest. It seems that at a point something deep down in them recognises the appeal and responds with obedience. I believe we should guard against passing sweeping negative judgments where the Holy Spirit of God has been at work.[33]

This is not to seek to diminish the failure of the Church to baptise African thought and experience into the unifying life of the Christian faith. Yet, with all the imperfections of the Church, it is the Word of God, not of man, that has been growing. True, it could have grown much more if in the past it had been given more freedom to touch the common life of African men and women. But it has begun to touch that life. Ordinary men and women, and of the first generation, have found the power of Christ in their lives stronger than their fear of witchcraft or the power of an old fetish shrine. Of an influential 'fetish' in the 1950s it was said: 'The important thing is not that Tigare does not exist, but that the power of Christ is far greater than Tigare.'[34] Extempore prayers, prayed in an evening prayer meeting, reveal a sense that God's presence in Jesus Christ as Lord has been with this man or that woman during the course of that day. The old, familiar name for God their fathers used is still used by them, but in a significant way magnified and deepened by the language and spirit of the New Testament. Above all, invoking the name of Jesus in circumstances similar to those in which would be used the name of the spirit at a local shrine reflects a new dimension of spiritual discernment and power.

4

The Challenges Facing the Church and the Principles of its Response

THE CHURCH, with the weaknesses and strengths we have examined, has the task of serving and challenging a revolutionary continent. In doing so, it faces the challenge of other strong movements of mind and spirit: Nationalism, Islam, Traditional Religion in old or new non-Christian forms, Secularism and Communism. For these encounters it is armed with the Christian faith as it has received it from the main religious tradition of the West. This tradition was smelted in the crucible of a different age and ethos: the crucible of Christianised Europe with a class-structured society based first on feudalism and eventually on democratic forms of capitalism. The institutions of the Church transplanted to Africa reflect the patterns of this Western tradition. Such a Church now has to come to grips in its own life and witness with quite other patterns of society and methods of government, such as African Socialism and single-party or non-party democracy.

NATIONALISM

Many names are used in an attempt to define the new life-

[63]

force that is coursing through the arteries of the continent in this generation: Nationalism, African Nationalism, Black Nationalism, Negritude, African Socialism. Under whatever term it is known, it is an overpowering force. Rulers and national leaders are seeking to direct it into constructive channels, yet only too often they find that it has taken charge and is directing them. The intelligent Christian recognises in this experience, this emotion, this driving force, a movement of the spirit of man which he believes is inspired by the God of history; and he cannot see its operation in recently independent countries without thanking God for the release of energy, the sense of purpose and opportunity, the common man's conviction that this is his age. Something much more is taking place than a series of palace revolutions. It is a people's movement, drawing its driving force from several sources: the awakened sense of the dignity of the dark-skinned peoples of the world; Socialist and Communist theories of the rights of the proletariat; the revolt of the East against Western political and economic imperialism; the influence, wherever the Christian Church has been true to its Lord, of teaching in the name of Him who said: 'You shall know the truth, and the truth will set you free.'[1]

A study group of the Tanzanian Christian Council refers to 'the sudden awareness of peoples' rights', and suggests that 'this awareness has produced a change in individuals both in speech and action. People feel that they have not only the right to speak but also the ability to speak and act.'[2] It is a social as well as a political revolution. This is revealed, for example, on meeting African women at international conferences and on UN delegations; or on seeing them at work in their own country as doctors, education officers, members of parliament, magistrates, bank clerks, policewomen, housewives, or on studying the influence they exert on social legislation, such as the recoding of their country's marriage laws.

This thrusting movement of the human spirit in Africa has to be given direction country by country, within the national boundaries inherited from the partition of the continent and the colonial era. The first duty of an independent government is to ensure the unity of the nation, to form a common allegiance from different tribal groups, with different languages and levels of economic development.

The cohesive strength of imperial power, exercised for one or more generations, vanished overnight, together with its symbols. The flag that was lowered had behind it economic and military might; the half-battalion of a famous regiment stationed in a colony had greater forces behind it at home. This strength of the colonial power remained a factor throughout the period of colonial administration, even if in its later stages—as was the case in many colonial territories on the eve of independence—it had been impossible to think of using that might against the known opposition of a whole people. The new flag that was raised had behind it at first little more than the negative, if unanimous, opposition to colonial rule. Critics who make much of the cult of the leader, the multiplying of public portraits, the cavalcades of motor-cyclist police, must consider the vacuum that existed both in symbol and reality. Amid the rejoicing within Ghana and without (maybe a little too patronising in the latter case) at the fall of a statue in Accra, the fact remains that something meaningful has still to be found to take its place.

'In virtually all of these [new nations] the first task of the new men of power is to create a new national identity that their fragmented people will recognise and accept.'[3] Behind these issues lies a deeper, as Max Warren reminds us: 'One of the basic problems confronting all the independent nations of Asia and Africa is that of finding an adequate substitute for the sanction of religion as the ultimate ground of governmental authority.'[4] In 1961, Edmund Ilogu wrote this of his country:

The picture we have drawn of Nigeria is that of a young nation not yet fortunate enough to have the unifying experience of one powerful ideology derived from a common religion or a long history of common suffering. It has not the cultural buttress of a common language, nor the over-all international leadership which has won the prestige that all citizens endeavour to uphold at all costs.[5]

Welbourn writes in the concluding chapter of his study of Uganda politics in the years 1952-62: 'Without an adequate mythology, neither a "Ugandan" identity nor an "East African" identity is possible; and no amount of manoeuvring, of repression or of forcible direction can create a politically viable unit out of a society which has no mythological unity.'[6]

The most immediate contribution of the Church in this issue of national identity, is to be, and be seen to be, a reconciling influence within the nation. Christians suddenly find that the clamant need of the nation throws a glaring light on their own disunity and that, to serve the community, they must the more urgently set their own house in order. Then standing as they do within a world-wide Christian fellowship, Christians have to wrestle with the tensions of national loyalty. 'No man is wholly Christian in the sense that he is free of the ties of a particular national culture, whether it is "British" or "Muganda"; no Briton or Muganda, who is also Christian, can commit himself wholly to his national culture.'[7] As the new African State experiences the pull between its own immediate self-interest and the concept of a wider fraternity, first in the Organisation of African Unity and then in the United Nations, so Christians experience the pull between the 'National' and the 'World' Church. The more the Church seeks to identify itself, to show the common man the way to God, the greater the danger of complete identification with his nationalism. African Christians, to whom the racially national identification of

European Christians has been so obvious, and so readily criticised, begin to grope in the dark themselves as the Sudan, Uganda, Togo, Ghana take on a national identity and become at odds with one another.

The forging of national unity, the making of a nation, is, then, the first task of independence. There are no long, slow years permitted for this. It has to be achieved within a time-scale dictated by two interlocking factors: the population explosion, and the increasing gap between rich and poor nations. In a very literal sense, the nations of Africa are young nations. Half the African population of Rhodesia is under seventeen years of age, as against approximately one-quarter in the United Kingdom. The 1963 population of Kinshasa of 750,000 or so will have doubled by 1980, apart from any further influx from the villages. The prominence of young teenagers in the Congo rebel forces in 1964 is a reminder that a significant part must be found quickly for this age-group in the new nation.

The second factor which allows governments no time is the economic difference between them and the industrial West. The oneness of the world through air travel, picture magazines, films, radio and television has opened up to village people what standards are possible in the world of which they, too, are citizens. They can no longer remain content with the ways of their fathers. Just as those of the author's generation, wishing that their mothers could have been saved back-aching Mondays with a scrubbing board at the copper, therefore put an electric washing-machine as first priority among modern aids for their wives, so the African husband asks now for tap-borne water to save those weary miles to the stream or well, and then raises his sights, and his wife's hopes, to the electric stove in place of the head-loading and chopping of firewood. And why should not the electric washer be just round the corner for his home, too?

In 1946, a Ghanaian just landed from an Elder Dempster boat after two years' post-graduate study in Britain spent the first evening back in his native land looking out over Sekondi from the wooden verandah of a friend's house. He saw the town, its lights and iron sheet roofs, stretched out before him. He could picture what was going on in those crowded rooms and compounds. His mind went to the London surburban home which had been his for many months past, and a great ache seized him. How many years, how many decades, how many lifetimes before what was commonplace in London would be so in Sekondi? And how much longer for his home village miles away?

His heart-ache, when translated into economic terms, spells capital formation and Professor W. Rostow's 'take-off into sustained growth'. How bring about the point of take-off? Can a generation, by taking thought, add that particular cubit to its capital formation which sets the chain reaction going? Can the nation be disciplined into postponing the demand for felt needs while the infrastructure is being prepared? 'Past saving has not taken place, yet the whole welfare state apparatus is felt as a need.'[8] Is the secret first to establish the nation's agriculture on a money economy, or to go as quickly as possible to heavy industry, even if raw materials have to be brought across the seas? With the time-factor spelled out on his desk by the latest census figures, the national leader who can keep a cool head amid conflicting economic theories is a leader indeed. And when the choice has been made and the first five-year plan is set in motion, the mass of the population—the youngsters crowding out of the top standards of the primary schools—have to be kept content until the results become apparent; and the claims by rural folk for a share of the promised utopia have to be protected from the pressure of the unemployed gangs of the town, the 'verandah boys', and the appetite of the bureaucratic elite.

With so much to do in so short a time, there must be a questioning of the best methods for government. Is the two-party system the best way of matching free discussion of differing points of view with economy of time and effort on the part of overburdened cabinet ministers? How to keep in balance 'national community, economic revolution and human rights'? Many African states are adopting a form of one-party government, claiming—as does Tanzania, for example—that this can provide ample room for choice of politicians and for discussion of viewpoints, of finding a synthesis, at the local level.

In the field of technology and technical training there is also a questioning of methods. The colonial powers were the privileged ones of history. Capital development, industrialisation and technical know-how came to them comparatively gradually. Can they understand, and can their methods of teaching reflect, the inescapable pressure on those who must plan similar development for their countries not in centuries but in decades? The very concept of a five-year plan associated with the industrial growth of Russia suggests that here is experience which new countries need to tap. Furthermore, if that experience proves to be valid, it would be a betrayal of a country's crying need to refuse to profit by it because of ideological associations.

★

These are the tasks of national leaders. What is the relation of the Christian Church and its worshipping congregations to the ferment of this nationalism, to this driving purpose, all this released energy and the colossal problems of its direction and satisfaction? Since the Church has been partly responsible for the national revolution, it now bears a new responsibility. Its task is both to help in sustaining the movement and to be its conscience. The right to the latter, a dangerous role, can only be earned through fulfilling the former. How, then, can the Church help to sustain the national enterprise?

First, by understanding the problems which face those in

[69]

government. There are Christian citizens in Africa who are competent economists, statisticians, agriculturists, lawyers, administrators, politicians, educators. These will make their professional contribution to national planning and its development, bringing to that contribution the integrity, sympathy and spiritual insight of their personal faith. What is required of the Church as a whole—through its leaders, ordained and lay—is something more general than this: a willingness on the part of those who are not trained in these separate disciplines to seek to gain a 'layman's' understanding of the issues involved. So some have studied together books like Guy Hunter's *The New Societies of Tropical Africa*; others have examined their country's white paper on economic planning or education. Having thus glimpsed the immense and staggering tasks facing their rulers and the far-reaching decisions they have to take, they go on to ask: 'What are the points which require explanation to our Church members as well as to our non-Christian neighbours?' 'Where are the points at which we are called as citizens actively to participate and, because of our calling as Christians, to give a lead to others?' 'Where have we—as a congregation or as individuals—to refrain from lavish, or even what seems to us essential, expenditure, if the urgent need of the country is for private savings towards adequate capital formation?' 'What changes in our traditional modes of living and working are required for the more adequate development of the national economy?'

In every town and village there are members of the local congregation who, by their own daily work in the home, on the farm, in the store or market, make up part of the sum total of the nation's endeavour. As M. M. Thomas writes of India: 'The Christian who worships in the local congregation is also a voter and may be also a member of a trade union or a chamber of commerce. He is a citizen as well as a Churchman and is called to relate the insights that he receives in worship, the love that is

Christ-formed in him, to the secular world in which he lives.'[9]
An experienced African civil servant, J. S. Annan, has written:
'The Church is called to inform society and act as the conscience of the nation.' It is when the Church has in such ways
as these 'informed', and only then, that it has the moral right to
use the divinely given responsibility to challenge the state, if
that prove necessary, on the methods used to achieve these ends
of national well-being. Annan continues: 'Christians have the
particular responsibility to see that the various programmes of
economic and technical development serve the real needs of the
people without unduly high cost in terms of moral, spiritual and
cultural values.'[10]

Some will say this is not the Church's business. The criticism
usually comes from two different sides. First, there are some
outside the Church who regard it as interfering; too often their
objection is only heard when it is their policies which the
Church is finding it necessary to criticise. Then there are those
in the Church who bring to it a pietistic tradition and interpretation of the Christian faith. For them the Church's concern is
spiritual, not material. The Church has often allowed itself to
be torn between two words of scripture: 'Give us today our daily
bread', and 'Man cannot live on bread alone'.[11] N. Berdyaev
points to the true synthesis and to the reason why the Church
must concern itself with things material—in this instance with all
the plans of the African State: 'My own daily bread is a material
problem; my brother's daily bread is a spiritual problem.'

If it should be necessary to challenge the State, there are two
parts to the homework the Church must do. Its leaders have to
seek guidance from those who are expert in the field concerned
so as to ensure that the proposed action by government has been
fully understood. They have also to enlist the help of their
theologians to ensure that the word the Bible says about man
and society applies to the problem under discussion. This level
of study is that which is planned in the new centres for the

Study of Church and Society proposed for several African countries, on the pattern of the Christian Institute for the Study of Religion and Society at Bangalore in South India. The task has hardly yet been begun. Paul Abrecht in an exceedingly relevant chapter of *The Churches and Rapid Social Change* writes:

> In most areas Christians have only begun to realise what this requires in terms of the preparation of leaders, of the education and training of the laity, and in relation even to the conception of the Church and its understanding of its function in the world. The tendency towards the one-party system is first of all a challenge to prepare itself for witness, to examine its own understanding of the nature of the political order.[12]

TRADITIONAL RELIGION

Throughout Africa there is belief in God the Creator. There is not always a shrine or priest dedicated to Him; more usually these are in the names of lesser gods regarded as nearer to the happenings of men's lives and with more power to avert danger when it threatens. Such threat can come through the wilful, unintended or unconscious breaking of the regulated pattern of life by the individual or the community, or through the malicious action of witchcraft. At the shrines, a sense of shame in regard to neglected social duties—both to present and past generations—is aroused, opportunity is afforded for confession and, through the acceptance of an offering, absolution is pronounced. Against lesser ills charms and amulets afford protection.

It is in the ritual of life itself, more than in liturgical worship, that the Creator is remembered; for here the context is the indivisible world of spirits created by Him: 'the ever-present spirits of the ancestors, whose constant contact with the life of man on earth brings the world of spirits so close to the land of the living'.[13] Unseen and seen are inextricably bound up in man's common experience. He is part of his wide-branching family, in which present and past cannot be separated. The sense of this oneness of experience, this religious living, is focused not so much in worship at shrines as in the ceremonies of naming, coming of age, marrying, burying, sowing, reaping.

The popularity of particular shrines rises and falls. Long treks are made to those whose reputation is currently strong, sometimes across national boundaries; yet the movements of peoples today tells against continuity of practice. Traditional religion may be less able than Islam and Christianity to survive the break-up of village life. Both Islam and Christianity offer a continuity of worship within which the sense of the oneness of the world of spirits can find its place. But in neither of these world-religions has there yet been achieved a theological interpretation of popular practice which accords with their orthodox presentation. In its proclamation of the Oneness of God, the Christian Church has pronounced against worship at the shrines of the lesser gods; but too little has been done to incorporate the seasonal ritual of the family in Christian rites.

The challenge of traditional religion to Christianity may not come through any new outright threat from the widespread growth of the cult of a particular shrine or god. Rattray's wistful words are not likely to be fulfilled:

I sometimes like to think, had these people been left to work out their own salvation, perhaps some day an African Messiah would have arisen and swept their Pantheon clean of the fetish (suman). West Africa might then have been the cradle of a new creed which acknowledged One Great Spirit, Who, being One, nevertheless manifested Himself in everything around Him and taught men to hear His voice in the flow of His waters and in the sound of His winds in the trees.[14]

[73]

Rather the challenge lies implicit in the deep levels of a people's psychology and their spiritual conception of the universe, in the need for cleansing from shame, in the need to hold within the worship of the Supreme Being the fellowship of the clan and the close relationship of the family. Unless this deeper challenge is met then Roland Oliver's reference (cited in chapter 3) to the Church dying at the centre becomes all too possible.

★

Only African Christians can take up this challenge. European missionaries knew their faith but did not enter African experience at the deeper level. Those who first criticised them for this knew the thought-world of their own people but were not sufficiently competent in the whole range of Christian thought. The Church in Africa has been waiting for those of its sons and daughters who have explored the fields of philosophy and psychology, who have studied Christian thinkers from the Fathers to the present day, and who at the same time have retained within their personal experience of the Father, the Son and the Holy Spirit that which entered their consciousness as children: their relation to the 'grandfathers' and the indivisibility of the family. These may more fully interpret the communion of the saints as subsuming the ancestors without robbing them of their identity, and more fully comment on 'God had made a better plan, that only in company with us should they reach their perfection'.[15] They will be required to answer the question posed by Father Bernard Clements in a sermon preached in Kumasi in 1927: 'And among the great crowds that collected last Sunday at Menhia to celebrate the Addei, the great day of the dead, will there not be a large element which will not find it difficult to learn of the fuller and more perfect observance of All Souls' Day, the Church's great Day of the Dead?'[16] At the consultation of African Theologians at Ibadan in January 1966, the Reverend Kwesi Dickson commended for study J. V. Taylor's words about the redemption of mankind: 'The Christian's link with his pagan ancestors, in remembrance and unceasing intercession, may be part of that ultimate redemption; for as Césaire, the Martiniquean poet puts it, "there is room for all of us at the rendezvous of victory".'[17] The Catholic bishops of Nigeria wrote in their Pastoral Letter on the occasion of national independence: 'The Communion of Saints embraces those African ancestors who have gone to heaven just as much as it does those who have been called the "holy pagans of the Old Testament". . . . The Christian Church is the greatest of all extended families, stretching out as it does to embrace the world and transcend the centuries.'[18]

The urgent unfinished task of theological understanding within the Church in Africa lies on the hearts and minds of a young generation of scholars. Its direction has by now been frequently described, as in the words quoted from K. A. Busia on page 50 above. Several contributors to the International African Institute's seminar on "The Impact of Christianity in Tropical Africa" held in Ghana in April 1965 pointed the same way. 'We have converted the mass of the people but not the communal conscience,' declares Father R. Bureau. He also speaks of 'a religious infra-consciousness which is no longer fully pagan, but which has not yet been baptised', and quotes a bishop as saying 'we manufacture Christians but life takes them away from us'. John Mbiti affirms that 'Christianity must deepen its roots in the context of our corporate community life, the soil wherein the Gospel is being planted'.[19] The task has been defined; theologians, laymen, pastors have to think and live and pray their way through it.

As has already been suggested in the section on Personal Experience in chapter 3, they are not starting completely from scratch. They have something on which to build. Certainly, among those who bear the name Christian, many experience an unbridged dichotomy; while a smaller number are the 'europeanised' of Williamson's description: those at home with the classics of the Christian devotional life. Between them is a not insignificant number who live in two worlds which, at the deeper level of prayer, are imperceptibly becoming one; they know that 'underneath are the everlasting arms', stronger than the power of witchcraft—indeed, already beginning in their subconscious to dissolve the reality of witchcraft; they do not in times of stress return to the old shrines; their faces light up as their lips pronounce the name 'Jesu'.

Whether those who will most fully respond to the challenge of traditional African religion will be found within the 'historic' or the 'independent' Churches it is not possible to prophesy. Much depends on the readiness of the 'historic' Churches to be 'born from spirit' and so be like the wind that 'blows where it wills' in forms of worship, healing ministries, theological expression and community life. Then there would be found, not only 'a religious practice which is Christian in function but African in form', but a Christian theology which has been enriched through the incorporation of spiritual insights, some of which the Western Church has forgotten or allowed to become overlaid.[20]

Yet perhaps it is in its ability to offer a new understanding of community that the faith which in its beginnings stressed fellowship (*koinonia*) will be most severely tested. Can it take up the words of Archbishop Zoungrana? 'Our forbears bequeathed us a concept of community which is based on spiritual values and respect for personal human rights. This African Socialism should be better understood and implemented.'[21] The poignant words of the old priest quoted by John Taylor from Monica Wilson's *Communal Rituals of the Nyakyusa* point the dilemma: 'If it were not for the ritual I would get you to speak to the Europeans of the Mission, and I would go with my wife, Jane, and be baptized ... I would like to go and be baptized with her. But I fear for the ritual, I fear hunger, the hunger of the people.'[22] And Taylor uses words from an earlier book of his to sum up:

> The question is, rather, whether in Buganda, and elsewhere in Africa, the Church will be enabled by God's grace to discover a new synthesis between a saving Gospel and a total, unbroken unity of society ... how to be in Christ without ceasing to be involved in mankind, how to be bound in the bundle of life, yet at one with the Lord their God.[23]

The part which university departments of Religious Studies can play in this creative study deserves mention. The older ones started as departments of Christian theology, but all have rightly now become departments of Religious Studies, where Traditional Religion, Islam and Christianity can be studied together. Fourah Bay, Legon, Ibadan, Nsukka and Makerere have proved to be active centres for the study of the Independent Churches, the gathering of local material for the writing of African Church history, and the systematic description of traditional religion. We still wait to receive from them equally sympathetic monographs on the spiritual experience of rank-and-file Christians within the historic Churches. The significance of the degree of African support for these departments should not be overlooked. They are not just the remnant of a European tradition kept alive by missionary influence, as the formation in 1966 of a new department at Ife proves. African witnesses stood up strongly to the questioning of those on the Elliott Commission in 1945 who were not in favour of a department of theology. When the Ghana department was under attack in the 1960 University Commission as something the country could not afford, the Russian member of the commission said nothing, Oxford and London attacked, Ghanaians said i must go on. Already these departments have provided the first generation of African Christian theologians with that freedom of academic time for research which the heavy demands of pastoral duties in their Churches had denied them. During the next few years the fruit of their lecturing and study should mark a break-through in the relation of the Christian faith to traditional religion.

ISLAM

Islam crossed the Sahara by the desert trade-routes. By early in the eleventh century, individual Negroes in the region of the Niger bend had become Muslims. The first forcible conversion came with the conquest of the old kingdom of Ghana from the north in 1076. By the time Mansa Musa, king of Mali, made his famous pilgrimage to Mecca in 1324, Islam had reached eastwards to Katsina and Kano in what is now Northern Nigeria. The great empires north of the forest belt broke down in the seventeenth and eighteenth centuries; during this period, Muslim traders and clerics were to be found in most towns, but the mass of the people remained Animists. The nineteenth century saw the development of 'theocratic' states with an emphasis on the uniqueness of Islam and its unwillingness to accept other worship alongside it. From the Wolof in Senegal to the Hausa in Nigeria and Cameroon, the islamisation of the common people became rapid, its consolidation being helped by the protective religious neutrality of the European occupation.

The policy of indirect rule in British West Africa added the authority of the colonial power to that of the Muslim ruler, thus making resistance to Islam on the part of Animists more difficult. Official protection for Islam as a religion became also a protective wall against the impact of Western cultural contacts. Lugard's successors put a more rigid interpretation, in respect to education as well as to religion, on his words: 'Government will in no way interfere with the Mohammedan religion.'[24] Margery Perham sums the issue up in a question that has relevance in independent countries today: 'If the receiving culture were indivisible, could the imposing culture be carved up for selective application?'[25] There was also the factor, hinted at by Victor Murray, that the policy was carried out in Northern Nigeria by Christian administrators from a public school tradition who leaned over backwards in their concern to be seen to be religiously impartial.[26]

The forest belt remained a barrier to Islam along much of the West African coast until very recently. Muslim traders or labourers were to be found to the south—as in Liberia, Ivory Coast and Ghana—but they made no religious impact on the coastal and forest peoples, and rarely proclaimed their presence through the building of a mosque. The one exception was in Nigeria, in the case of the Yoruba. In the past thirty years, however, the rate of penetration has been much greater— albeit more through the movement of northern Muslims into permanent settlement in the coastal towns than through conversion. In most of these towns today a mosque is a common sight. At the same time, there has been a movement starting from the coast with the help of Pakistani missionaries of the Ahmadiyyah sect. Beginning in 1921, though building in Lagos and Saltpond on earlier local orthodox Muslim groups, the Ahmadiyyah have spread along the coast in English-speaking countries. Humphrey Fisher's survey showed that its converts had come from orthodox Muslims and Christians, and hardly at all—perhaps 5 per cent—from pagans.[27] A more recent examination of the record-cards of new members of the Saltpond headquarters shows two-thirds previously Christian and one-third Animist.[28]

In East Africa, the spread of Islam had two distinct stages. Initially, islamisation by Arab and Persian traders of the coastal fringe and the islands from Mogadishu to Sofala resulted in the founding of Swahili culture groups in the thirteenth and fourteenth centuries. These made practically no religious impact on the Bantu in East Africa, until the shake-up of East African society when European trade and then rule spread into the interior. Then Islam struck roots in a few areas for various reasons—one being that the new man of prestige, the European, recruited all his guides, servants, police and carriers from among the Muslims of the coast. With few exceptions, these areas were limited to the trade-routes through to Lake Tanganyika and, southwards, to the Yao in what is now Tanzania, Malawi and Mozambique. This expansion into the interior was at its most vigorous between 1880 and 1930.

The faith of Islam centres in the morning and evening prayers, the Friday prayer, and the annual fast of Ramadan: these strengthen and help to institutionalise the faith of the convert. Air travel makes it possible for large numbers to make the pilgrimage to Mecca. Only in the East African coastal settlements has islamisation meant the acceptance of a different culture. For the rest—Bantu and West African Negro alike—becoming Muslim has not meant any radical change in social life. 'Islam was received purely as a religion and it has not broached African Negro social structures; this distinguishes it from the total Islam of the Berber Arabs which penetrated all their institutions and which cannot be separated from Arab civilisation.'[29] In sub-Saharan Africa, there was therefore little change in the world view or in social customs. Amulets were accepted; as Fisher remarks: 'The amulet is the most convertible currency in West African religion.'[30] Polygamy was acceptable. In theory, ancestor relationships were not acceptable, nor were secret societies. Trimingham's comment on the position relating to both Muslims and Christians in West Africa, across Sierra Leone and Guinea applies elsewhere too: 'The break-up of traditional religions is apparent everywhere, as is the fact that the abandonment of their African religious heritage is only partial and that the springs of conduct of those who have joined one or other of the two available world religions is still that of the old animistic heritage.'[31]

★

Which of the two, Islam or Christianity, can most readily provide the institutional basis for African traditional religion within the demands of national self-expression?

The advantages seem at first sight to be with Islam. It makes less demand for change than Christianity in regard to polygamy and in regard to charms and amulets. It offers a more readily seen brotherhood, both in community welfare and in a unity that crosses tribal boundaries. Just as Islam enhances the personal dignity of the labourer from the north as he lives among the southern Akan in Ghana, so amid racial pressures Cassius Clay has found what white Christianity has often denied. Christians in Freetown and Lagos frequently have the apartheid of South Africa thrown at them by Muslims. (Blindness to that denial of equality which is inherent in racial segregation in South Africa and Rhodesia may yet be the most important factor in the rejection of the Christian faith in Africa, not least in those countries themselves.) But perhaps the most immediately potent advantage with Islam lies in its doctrine of the Islamic State. To the leader seeking national unity, the idea of an Islamic State rather than one neutral towards religion has great attractions; the pressure is felt when he consorts with heads of state from North Africa. Recent events in Northern Nigeria, the Northern Cameroon and the Sudan indicate some of the politico-social pressures on large Animist communities to become Muslim.

On the other hand, Islam has been slow in the past at welcoming westernisation. There is still a dearth of educational facilities in most Muslim as compared with Christian or mainly

[81]

Animist areas. And Islam as well as Christianity faces the effect of secularisation. Trimingham makes a similar comment in regard to both East and West Africa, noting that the effect of secularisation is to restrict and narrow the sphere in which Islam can mould the lives of its adherents.[32]

The question: Islam or Christianity? has to be answered in the context of a technological world. Both have to interpret their message and their life in this new situation, and be able to offer a satisfying answer to the need of townspeople for a new sense of community. The indications are that Christians are asking the more searching questions about their faith; but there is no room for complacency. Much depends on the degree to which the Christian Church can be true to the teaching of its Lord, finding again its unity, serving in the world of tomorrow as He served. Above all, it must be true to His teaching and example in its presentation of the Gospel to Muslims.

The shadow of the crusades still lies darkly across attempts by Christians to talk with Muslims about their faith. Even in West Africa, there is a history of implacable denunciation and denigration on the part of Christian preachers where there should have been love. The road that love requires, that of service and dialogue, is a difficult one to travel. To hold to the conviction that in Jesus Christ God spoke uniquely to men and that the salvation He wrought was meant for all men, and yet patiently to talk, seeking to understand the other man's faith and the reality of his worship—this calls for a patience and a wisdom which are not always natural gifts. It is an approach which some Christians do not feel strong enough in their own faith to attempt; in the eyes of some of their fellow-Christians, it is regarded as betrayal.

The White Fathers have sought to commend Christ to Muslims through service in medicine and agriculture in North and West Africa. Men have done this for a lifetime in Algeria, never in all that time baptising anyone, yet living in the community as those who serve. That this service has left its mark is seen in the simple story of the Muslim pall-bearers at the funeral of one of the Fathers after his murder by an Arab gang during the Algerian war of independence. Yet the Word become flesh reflected in a life of service today must at some point be put into words. The study given by the White Fathers to the history, doctrine and piety of Islam prepares the way for dialogue.

Recently, through a small number of advisers, the 'Islam in Africa Project' has been working in this way among a number of Protestant Churches.* Its aim is 'To aid the Church in Africa in its encounter with Islam by offering it help in understanding the disciples of Muhammad and in proclaiming to them the Gospel of Jesus Christ.' First comes a study of Islam and the Koran, then a study of the New Testament, leading to discussion with Muslims: a discussion which seeks to find the large amount of common ground between them, but does not hide what the Christian has found in his acceptance of the Christian revelation. It is a growing process, for true dialogue leaves neither participant the same man as when it began. 'In our encounter with Muslims we are constantly driven to learn and relearn for ourselves what the Gospel is.'[33] For the more thorough study of the Christian way in presenting the Gospel to Muslims, a study centre has been set up in Ibadan, named after one who was its inspiration—the late Pierre Benignus. He knew that preaching failed if Christ was not seen in the preacher's life, and endorsed Trimingham's words: 'We need to remember that the attitude of Christians towards Islam largely determines the attitude of Muslims towards Christianity. Christians and Muslims, neighbours on the material plane, have yet to learn the things that belong to their peace.'[34]

* A Liaison Committee, directed from the Pierre Benignus Study Centre at Ibadan, Nigeria, was set up following a Consultation on Islam in Africa held in Holland in September 1958.

SECULARISM

In company with the rest of the world, Africa is experiencing the rapid secularisation of life which is involved in the technological revolution. Electronic control in the new factories, computers in government offices, the harnessing of waterpower in massive hydroelectric installations—all confirm man in the control of his environment. Even in the village, man's part in the success of the harvest has been multiplied by mechanical irrigation, tractors, chemical fertilisers and insecticides. The need for the concept of God and of the miraculous to explain the successive acts in the process recedes further and further away. At the same time, man and woman become subject to the depersonalising factors of modern production and succumb to harsh competition among themselves to obtain its material output, treading one another down in the drive to be 'carfull and fridgefull'. Already African society is finding that what is welcomed for the greater freedom it offers has within it possibilities of deeper enslavement. The twenty-four hours' round-the-clock servicing of a power-station and the second-hand of a broadcasting studio clock break into the concept of 'time to spend with people' on the way to the farm or under the village elders' tree.

Yet to lament the 'timelessness' of the village is not the answer. The mills of Bombay have banished Gandhi's dream of a cottage-spinning industry in India, and are a reminder that nostalgia and romanticism are not the way to ensure that what is at the heart of the old values will survive. Secularisation has to be welcomed for the good that is in it. This need not be a surrender to secularism: 'a way and an interpretation of life that include only the natural order of things and that do not find God or a realm of spiritual reality essential for life or thought'.[35]

This surrender has happened for many in the West. Rena

Karefa-Smart has spoken of secular materialism as 'the unconscious missionary faith of the West'. This interpretation of technology and life is that which is most often reflected in the films, advertisements, literature and broadcasts of the West. It is not the only interpretation possible for the secularised life. Theism can accept secularisation and still recognise God in the basic acts of creation and in the creation and sustaining of man. The Christian faith sets forth the Christ who said 'I am come that man may have life, and may have it in all its fullness'.[36] It still sees Him when it has accepted the secular to the full: 'For though everything belongs to you ... yet you belong to Christ, and Christ to God.'[37] Or again: 'The whole universe has been created through Him and for Him.'[38] The working out of this faith in practice, the preservation of spiritual values—or rather, the active response in a secular age to the Spirit of God—calls for an active and costly outreach of mind and spirit.

★

Secularism as an ideology, whether materialistic or humanistic, offers little challenge to Christianity or Islam in Africa at the moment. To village life, atheism has no meaning and no appeal. African thought does not conceive of the world apart from God. In the words of a Muslim thinker in Mali, Amadou Hampati Ba: 'Without God, nothing will succeed in Africa.' This is still the common faith of townspeople. Is this because they are Africans with 'an African's deep sense of the spiritual'; or is it that, unlike so many of their European and American counterparts, they are as yet only one generation removed from the manually worked farm, with its reminder of forces other than man's which co-operate in producing the work of his hands? Is there not already apparent in a few that erosion of faith which in another generation can become secularism? On the other

[85]

hand, African spirituality may prove stronger than European and, in return for the art of technology, may reveal to Europe and America the secret of retaining theism as the basis of a technological society.

The offer of the Christian faith as an answer to secularism will be effective only as the Church shows clearly its acceptance of secularisation. This implies a welcome to technology, industrialisation, bureaucratic government and to the physical, mental and spiritual well-being of man these can promote. If such welcome is to be positive, and not mere acquiescence, Christians will have to study these movements and the sociology resulting from them. Only thus can there be offered, to the individuals and families moulded by them and living together in the new patterns they require, personal service by Christian neighbours and opportunities for corporate recreative worship by the Christian community in forms and patterns which have meaning and which throw light on the purposes of God in secular life.

That the Church in Europe and America is painfully slow in this regard in its own community, being tied to patterns of congregation and ministry, church building and ecclesiastical structure, which militate against meeting modern man within the pattern of his life, does not exonerate the Church in Africa from fulfilling its responsibility. Even there, against the background of so much that is still the busy life of village people, the question presses: Is there so much time? Is there any fundamental difference in the need for friendship and service and the 'good word said for Jesus Christ' of the Londoner who stands on his way home in the crowded 5.31 from Victoria, of the Orlando traveller from Johannesburg Central, and of the Lagos worker from Surulere suburb in the rush-hour traffic jam on Carter Bridge? The Church has to enter into the developing technological society so as to offer new concepts of community based on a spiritual understanding of secular life. With the disintegration of tribal life, the traditional built-in social security system is also disappearing. The answer of Christians is to offer a spirit-guided fellowship set free from out-moded structures: a fellowship in which worship, especially the communion of the Lord's Supper in someone's 'upper room', and mutual service are one.

COMMUNISM

Just as with secularism, Communism—in so far as it is atheistic —is not as great a challenge to Christianity in Africa as in the West. Its challenge lies rather in the area of offered equality in those countries where men seek a quick path to the achievement of egalitarianism, whether in face of racial discrimination or economic poverty.

When racial discrimination is at issue, it is ironically those white people who are most insistent that their countries are a bastion for Christian civilisation against Communism who are most patently opening the door to it by their own actions and policies. The words of Chief A. Luthuli are on record. Of Communism he has said: 'Communism seems to me to be a mixture of a false theory of society linked to a "false" religion. . . . In religion I am a Christian.'[39] Alongside this must be put his words at the Freedom Trial when challenged with having been an associate of Communists: 'Now we don't know Communism; all we know is that these men and women came to us to help us. I don't deny that some might have ulterior motives; all I am concerned about is that they came to assist us in fighting racial oppression; and they have no trace of racialism or of being patronising—just no trace of it at all.' It has been said of French-speaking West Africa that the left wing has won the trust of Africans by behaving in ways that Africans have never seen Europeans behave; they were personal friends and comrades, rather than Europeans.

There may be contrary evidence from the experience of races

which make up the Soviet Union; that is not to the point here. What remains crystal clear is that the Christian Gospel is rejected by many Africans today because those of European race, in Africa and outside, claim the name of Christ but do not do His works: their practice of racial segregation and acquiescence in unequal opportunities for the races being in fact a denial of fellowship in Christ. This is the strongest challenge of Communism to Christianity in Africa today. Those who point this out are sometimes accused of pressing racial integration on others—e.g. in Rhodesia, Angola, South Africa—in order to promote the missionary enterprise elsewhere in the continent. They must still support what they see to be the truth, even if this gloss is put on their actions.

★

When that which attracts a Communistic answer is the presence of economic poverty, then there is real possibility of external Communist influence. Cruel and wasteful of human spiritual and physical resources as the process has been, the major Communist countries have set a practical example of planned development from illiteracy, widespread poverty and a largely peasant and agricultural economy, to universal education and industrialisation. Hence Dr Nyerere refers to China, not so much as a country whose ideology he approves, as one whose solutions of parallel problems with those of Tanzania seem more relevant and feasible of emulation by his people than anything the affluent nations have to offer.

The Church is already seen as apparently accepting affluent status in the West. It will become vulnerable in Africa if exclusively allied with the emerging middle class of African society. Dr A. Aluko of Nigeria says that Christians 'should recognise that it is the revolt of the people against injustice which gives Communism much of its strength. They should seek

[88]

to recapture for the Churches the original Christian solidarity with the distressed peoples.'[40]

The attempts by both Russian and Chinese governments to introduce Communist ideology into African states through diplomatic and economic missions are well-documented. The only satisfactory answer is to eliminate the causes which make such an ideology attractive. Europe and America have to recognise the need for a common market crossing all boundaries, and to respect the African desire for non-alignment. Indeed, the lesson the Church is so slowly learning itself in regard to the mission of the Gospel has something to teach the exponents of political ideologies, namely, that disinterested service is the best commendation of a way of life, that 'he who would save his life must lose it'.

★

Much of what has been written in this chapter of the Christian response is ideal in that only in small part is it being achieved: the Church filling out the content of nationalism; extending the deep experience of traditional religion; offering fellowship to Muslims; accepting courageously the implications of secularisation, itself contributing to and pressing for racial and economic justice. What, in the present life of the Church in Africa—institutionally and through its individual members, in its corporate witness and study and in the daily living of Christians—is being done towards these ends?

5

The Intellectual Response

WHEN THE VATICAN Council was discussing the first, rather
conservative, draft of the schema on 'the Church' a voice
expostulated on behalf of the African bishops: 'They had expected a joyful announcement of the good news that was the
Church. . . . The Church was here described as a static entity,
whereas it was a living body. . . . The people of Africa were
looking for a new manner of living together as a community—a
new solid, holy way of life.'[1]

This voice—and others such as the twin voices from
Cameroon, Archbishop Zoa at the Vatican Council and Pastor
Jean Kotto at the World Council of Churches—is the voice of
the Church of Christ in Africa. Despite all that remains to be
achieved, despite past failures and lost opportunities, despite the
challenge of Islam and Secularism, despite all the uncertainty
of achievement of the new nation-states of Africa, and amid the
greater uncertainty of a catastrophic outcome of the atomic age
inaugurated by the first splitting of the atom by Rutherford and
the first atomic bombardment at Hiroshima by the Western
powers, these voices suggest that the Church can be significant
in independent Africa. In this and the following chapter,
glimpses will be attempted of thought and action in the name

of the Church, however frail some of it is. They are chosen from here and there with no attempt to catalogue or be exhaustive They may in total be seen to be pointers, indicative of life and movement, and so may enable us to attempt an answer to the question raised at the beginning of this book: What of the Church in the Africa of the future?

★

Archbishops Zoungrana of Ougadougou and Rugambwa of Bukoba made distinctive contributions to the Vatican Council. Sixty-one black African bishops were there among the 2,500. By 1965, the sixty-one had become seventy, two of them cardinals. In all, the Roman Catholic Church today has something like 2,500 African priests. For the first three decades of this century, the Roman Catholic Church seemed to be lagging behind the Protestant Churches in the number of African priests and Church leaders. But the long quiet years of the seminary course were being fulfilled, so that when African priests began to take their place in increasing numbers alongside missionary priests, their training was such as enabled them quickly to move into positions of responsibility. Admittedly, patterns of training to achieve this equality laid more emphasis on the study of canon law in Rome than on anthropology and sociology, but this balance is being rectified. It is true that the proportion of African to missionary priests is as yet only one to six, and reference has already been made to the worsening position of the over-all proportion of clergy to laity. Yet in an increasing number of African countries, when the chief representative of the Catholic Church speaks in the name of the Catholics of his country, it is a national speaking. This is so in Mali, Ghana, Guinea, Senegal, Cameroon, Tanzania, Uganda, Lesotho, Dahomey, Ivory Coast, Madagascar, Togo. Similar lists could be drawn up for the heads of the Protestant Churches and, in particular, for the secretaries of the various National Christian Councils. Significantly today, the Methodist Church of Rhodesia, with its considerable white membership, speaks officially through a black Rhodesian.

This African voice is already speaking in the idiom of the country, not only in the use of the vernacular in worship but also in music. The Missa Luba has been in regular use in the Congo for several years. Local settings to the Psalms are in use in Cameroon. In two articles in *Flambeau,*[2] the Abbé Pre-Claude Ngoumou describes first the background and then the principles which govern these compositions. The Abbé makes his case in the first article by devoting two-thirds of its length to a simple and moving account of the daily life of a village family such as that in which he himself grew up. Artlessly he reveals the part played in it by rhythm, music and dancing. He then asks: 'Is it necessary to rob him of these essential living realities of his life in order to baptise him and incorporate him in Christ?' In a lecture given to Protestant theological students in Yaoundé, the Abbé showed how in Cameroonian Catholic circles there had been a gradual development from the use of African vocal music, through the use of certain African musical instruments as well, to the use of even those instruments which had the most clearly secular associations. (Incidentally, this latter stage points to two sides of africanisation: an openness on the part of Christians to use, and a readiness on the part of the community to allow to be used, what had traditionally been reserved for specific purposes.) This account from Cameroon shows a Church not only experimenting at certain professional levels but with its members already at ease in the medium. From Cameroon, too, comes word of the practice of the Clarist Sisters in Sangmelima dancing before the Eucharist in the Church.[3] Reference can also be made to a conference on African Liturgical Music for Xhosa-speaking dioceses held in December 1965. Among the Protestants, there has been since

1962 an annual workshop in Church music at the Mindolo Ecumenical Foundation in Zambia, serving eastern and southern countries in Africa. One result was the formation in 1963 of the All-Africa Church Music Association. The aim of the workshops has been to produce hymns from traditional music with African words. The systematic acceptance of these new forms is not yet as advanced with Protestant as with some Roman Catholic congregations.

In no part of life is the test of the ability of the Christian faith to become relevant more decisive than in the home. In recent years, at continental and national level, no subject has received more attention from both Catholics and Protestants. In the Catholic Church, National Family Apostolate movements have developed in a number of countries, such as the Mouvement Familial Chrétien of Congo and the Christian Family Movement of Zambia. Local membership is sometimes through married couples, who meet in quite small groups to share the problems of bringing up children and of husband-wife relationships. In other cases, husbands and wives meet in separate groups. They take as their guide in this mutual sharing the motto, 'Observe, Judge, Act'. International conferences have been held, such as that of the Action Catholique des Familles, with representatives from nine French-speaking countries, at Cotonou in August 1962. Among the issues discussed have been: the enhancement of the status of women; the education of women and girls; dowry and payments in connection with marriage; remote and immediate preparation for marriage; the liberty of widows; inheritance; housing.

On the Protestant side, an important seven weeks' consultation was held at Mindolo in Zambia early in 1963, with representatives from fifteen countries—mostly married couples who could on their return home together serve the Churches of their country through the Christian Council. The subjects studied were very much those listed above: customary marriage; bride price; polygamy; Christian marriage; family planning; the unmarried life; Christian home and family life programmes; Church discipline; divorce; prostitution. Consultants were present on the theological, sociological, educational and medical aspects of the study. The degree of confidence in discussing these issues within the study group between husband and wife, men and women, Africans and Europeans, grew as the weeks passed. Conferences of many more people meeting for a shorter time could not have achieved what this seminar did either in its report or in the work of the participants on their return home.[4] In Yaoundé in Cameroon, the couple who attended the Mindolo Seminar have worked full time for more than two years in Christian home and family work. This has comprised discussion with youth groups, women's groups, secondary schools, theological college students, together with visitation of homes where there are difficulties. Personal counselling has been given to husbands and wives in trouble, to couples seeking advice in establishing and maintaining a Christian home, to girls differing from their fathers about their marriage (usually concerning the amount of the dowry), to parents discouraged by the conduct of their children. Just normal pastoral work, yet significant in that it is done by a lay couple, themselves with quite a large family. The Ghana Christian Council runs three medical advice centres for married couples. These have saved some marriages from breaking up when threatened by continued childlessness. The 'Christian Home Week' programme of this Council has had as recent themes: the need for less expensive family occasions at marriages and funerals, and teenage problems. Voluntary conferences for teachers on sex teaching in schools are held in different parts of the country and are linked to specially prepared syllabuses for use in middle and secondary schools.

★

This measure of common thinking between Protestants and Catholics in the sphere of home and family life is seen also in the Churches' thinking about nationalism and national economic needs. The Catholic method of study is for the material to be put forward in pastoral letters by the bishops. These pastorals then form guidance for the laity and its material for study. Three such pastorals may be mentioned: *Shaping our National Destiny*, Uganda 1962; *Unity and Freedom in the New Tanganyika*, 1960; *The Catholic Church in an Independent Nigeria*, 1960. The Tanzania pastoral is a tightly reasoned statement of thirty pages on Church and State in a pluralistic society. It sets forth for Catholics their duty as an apostolate in such a society; their mission to share the truth has to be fulfilled in a context of respect for the convictions of others and through service to them. 'Only by living in the midst of our fellowmen, and showing practical interest in their welfare, can we hope each of us to become in some small measure the "salt of the earth", the "light of the world".' The Nigeria pastoral goes into greater detail concerning a wide range of the Church's concerns: social problems; nepotism and bribery; industrial relations; Christian marriage; a Nigerian clergy; liturgy and the Bible; the Church in a multireligious society. 'It may be asked why the Catholic Church should take a stand on social issues as well as on directly spiritual ones. The answer is simple. St Augustine wrote many centuries ago that "the life of the saints is a social one". Nobody can be a true member of the Church who is not a good citizen of the state.' The laity need study groups: 'There is no good reason why a man's knowledge of Christian doctrine should halt for good half-way through secondary school.' There is recognition of the nation's employment and economic problems:

Very soon the extension of primary education will see hundreds of thousands of Primary School leavers emerging

[96]

into the labour market. . . . It may well be that for our democratic system it is a race against time between the progressive raising of our standards of living and the discontent that may tempt some of our people to turn to authoritarian short-cuts. . . . We are also worried lest those who draw salaries from the government should go on being favoured at the expense of the vast but as yet inarticulate section of the country composed of the farming communities.

The Protestant method has been to call representative conferences of ministers and laymen, whose reports have then become study material for local congregations. Since 1948, such conferences on an all-Africa basis have usually been arranged by, or in association with, the organisation of Protestant Churches known as the All-Africa Conference of Churches (AACC). An account of the formation of this Conference and the consultations it has sponsored will be found in Appendix III. In what follows, certain major conferences are referred to by the name of their meeting-place: Ibadan 1958; Kampala 1963; Enugu 1965; Nairobi [Youth] 1962.

When it comes to the theme of so many of the Roman bishops' pastoral letters—the Church and Nationalism—all of these Protestant conferences reflect a concern for involvement; their theological argument provides support for involvement in the world and not withdrawal. 'To be a Christian in this time and place means to be fully engaged in the whole of African life', declared the Youth Assembly at Nairobi.[5] The sense of the Ibadan, Nairobi and Kampala conferences was given at Enugu by a speaker who proclaimed: 'We rejoice in the political freedom of the people of our continent.'[6] The Church was seen at Ibadan as having a threefold function: prophetic, educational and pastoral. 'To uphold righteousness, champion the oppressed, and declare the sovereignty of God over all creation including the institutions of man'; 'to provide education

[97]

in Christian citizenship'; 'to give true pastoral care to those of its members who are called to take an active part in the politics of their country.' There was as yet no felt need to grapple with the fact of one-party governments; the conference called 'for vigilance wherever self-government is achieved lest any [basic human] rights be impaired, including the right of constitutional opposition within and without the legislature'.[7]

Five years later, at Kampala, the threefold task of the Church was stated rather differently: prophetic, reconciling, witnessing. 'A "Watchman" in the midst of a nation, prophetically witnessing to the Divine demands for truth, justice and peace, and against all forms of oppression, discrimination, injustice and corruption'; 'witness to the reconciliation which is in Jesus Christ where there is conflict'; 'to witness by her own life and example the love and peace which she commends to the nations.'[8] Kampala became more deeply involved in the meaning of Nationalism and its outworking. It faced the question of political party membership and of the possibility of a one-party system. 'We recognise that in the interests of cohesion and national unity the one-party system might be acceptable; but the inherent danger of dictatorship must be guarded against.'[9] There was more realism in debate. A resolution moved from the floor, condemning the governments of South Africa, Angola, and Mozambique for repression of minority opinion and violation of basic human rights, was debated for more than half an hour. Omit names, said a delegate from one of the countries named. No, moved the conference, your country cannot get away with it so easily. Then amendments were suggested: 'add Sudan', 'add Ghana', 'add Southern Rhodesia'—but not by nationals of those countries. The conference began to have second thoughts. Delegates did not question the claim that other names be added; they began to see from within their own countries that the task of the Church there in challenging just these injustices might be made more difficult by this public listing. In the end, a positive resolution setting out certain fundamental human rights was adopted, but not associated with the name of any country. When two years later, at Enugu in 1965, a not dissimilar resolution was moved, a West African delegate at once rose and said: 'If you include that country you should also include mine.' Within five minutes on this occasion, an adequate resolution was drafted and approved.

These appraisals reflected the experience of the Church in the countries themselves. On some of the gravest points of disagreement between the Church and the State since independence, there may in some countries be on record no outspoken *resolution* of Synod or Christian Council that can be quoted as setting out the fundamental position of the Church. The records will show instead some fearless interviews at the highest level—insisted on by Church leaders—in which plain words were spoken, and in consequence of which a retreat from a position taken up by government was effected because there had been no hardening of position due to public outcry. This is a road fraught with dangers, and where the government concerned has been European, as in Rhodesia, one which Africans have strongly criticised. There may well be differences of method called for as between a situation where there is a large racial majority under the oligarchic rule of another race, and one in which the oligarchy is of the same race as the majority.

In another facet of the problem of racial minority rule the later conferences of the AACC were not afraid to discuss the use of force. The Kampala report (1963) has this paragraph:

One of the essential and urgent issues raised for Christians in relation to nationalism is the use of violence. Several different convictions were expressed. Some believe that Christians should refuse violence under all circumstances, and witness only through suffering. Some believe that the use of violence as an ultimate course of action is legitimate when the established authorities are instruments of injustice and oppression, and provided that such violence is exercised in an organised fashion and is likely to lead to the establishment of a better order of justice and freedom. All agreed that the indiscriminate use of violence for the achievement of collective vengeance or personal ends is never justified.[10]

A conference at Mindolo in 1964 on race relations in Southern Africa said: 'For many Christians involved in the struggle for a just solution, the question of possible violence as the only remaining alternative has become an urgent and ever-pressing one.'[11] The report goes on to list the forms of resistance to evil in government: first, spiritual resistance through prayer; next, legal forms of political opposition where still available; third, where legal forms fail, illegal forms may become necessary; finally, 'there is a growing feeling, even among men of responsibility and of Christian faith, in favour of the use of force to end what they feel to be the *impasse* in Southern Africa'.[12] Consultation then took place to discuss what positive actions to bring reconciliation across racial barriers were still possible, and to urge their active pursuit.

The references to thinking in a Christian context about forceful resistance to oppression are made here to indicate that Christians in Africa are not merely skirting the fringe of the problems facing them. At this point they find themselves in opposition to careful European experience which puts all the emphasis on law and order even when that law and order involve what governed Africans regard as injustice, and their rulers when honest admit as such. Paul Verghese reflects African thought in words spoken at Nairobi: 'I am not afraid of uncontrolled power coming up for a while. The framework of law and order will slowly be imposed on that power. But if you are going to put the framework of law and order before things come up, then they will kill the whole power. So I do not want the framework of law and order to be an obstacle to the release of these creative forces.'[13] In another context he writes: 'Freedom could not have emerged in Western Europe if the primary concern had been for non-violence, law and order. Some lessons have to be learned by experience.'[14]

At Enugu in 1965, the function of the Church was spelled out at three levels: 'the Church as an institution, speaking through its assemblies; the Church as a people forming part of a larger community; the Church as Christian laymen dispersed in the different activities of nation building'. At each of these levels, the same threefold function spoken of at Ibadan and Kampala should be exercised: reconciling, prophetic, serving. Enugu replaced Kampala's 'witness' by 'service'. There need be no contrast here for, in words used by the Reverend E. A. Adegbola at Enugu: 'Worship, Evangelism and Service, these three elements constitute together our witness to Christ. Each stands in its own right and must be held together in the fellowship of the common life which the Holy Spirit creates. . . . Evangelism which does not spring out of the Church's common life and love expressed in service will become mere empty sound.'[15]

There was also examination at Enugu of the involvement of the Church in the day-by-day working of national plans. While the Church's major contribution of an earlier date—education and medicine—became increasingly integrated in over-all State planning, the individual units were specifically Church-related. Pupils and patients entered the domain of the Church on entering school and hospital, however much that school and hospital were felt to be part of the community. The change in thinking, away from institutional to individual involvement, has taken place slowly. Little was said explicitly at the Ibadan conference. At Kampala, there was a clearer statement:

In the situation of a changing society ... Christians must learn to work with non-Christians in the development of community life and the furthering of community welfare. This means:

1. That the Churches must show in their own programmes of community service their concern for the welfare of all peoples, and

2. That they and their members must be prepared to work with non-Christians in common efforts of community welfare and development.[16]

It is in the older service of education that creative thinking along these lines is most urgently called for. The continent-wide consultations on education, at Salisbury in 1962 for Protestants and at Kinshasa in 1965 for Catholics, have stated the issues. Control of schools by the Churches should not be retained merely for its own sake but for reasons that are valid in each particular instance. As a Roman Catholic contributor to a discussion on education in Africa held at Chicago in 1964 put it: 'The Church must concentrate more on training sailors than on just building boats.'[17] In this task of training, the Churches in Africa have been greatly assisted in recent years by teachers recruited on direct appointment by the Overseas Appointments Bureau of the Christian Education Movement and by Catholic Overseas Appointments.

Among the continent-wide consultations on specific subjects arranged by the AACC have been: Urban Africa (Nairobi 1961), Literature and Audio-Visual (Mindolo 1961), Education (Salisbury 1962), Independent Church Movements (Mindolo 1962), Home and Family Life (Mindolo 1963), Women's Status and Responsibility in Church and Society (Kampala 1963), the Evangelisation of West Africa Today (Yaoundé 1965), Biblical Revelation and African Belief (African theologians, Ibadan 1966), the Christian Presence in the University (Accra 1966).

Parallel with these consultations on an all-Africa basis, regional and national discussions and study were proceeding. Some owed their inspiration to the All-Africa Conference of Churches or to the World Council of Churches, others to the already existing interchange of thought provided by the Christian Council of a country. Several studies were related to the World Council's study of the Church in Areas of Rapid Social Change. One such local study was undertaken in 1960 by the Nigeria Christian Council and published as *Christian Responsibility in an Independent Nigeria*. This report makes interesting parallel reading to the Nigerian bishops' pastoral letter (cited on page 96 above). The themes of Ibadan are repeated: the Church and Society; the Church and Political Life; Economic and Social Change; Church Growth and Evangelism; Christian Unity: Relationships among Protestant Churches; Christian Unity: Protestant–Roman Catholic Relationships; Indigenisation. A more recent study in Tanzania on one aspect only of rapid social change—Urban Situations—is found in the report *The Church Meets Life in the Town*.[18] In this whole field, the survey published in 1961 by the Reverend Paul Abrecht, *The Churches and Rapid Social Change*, which covers Asia and Latin America as well as Africa, is a textbook still to be fully discovered by African Christians.

One major aspect of rapid social change, urbanisation, is vigorously discussed throughout Africa. The Ibadan conference drew attention to the problems arising from the rapid growth of towns, but did not suggest any lines along which solutions might be found. The first post-Ibadan consultation was that at Nairobi in March 1961 on the mission of the Church in urban Africa. If there was little that was specifically African in the report, a number of working pastors from town parishes had shared their problems and faced certain principles. They recognised their own lack of training for work with towns-people, the need to understand the changes taking place around them and in the structure of industry and industrialised society, the necessity of challenging existing patterns of worship and congregation, and the need for team work and for crossing denominational boundaries. This was a working consultation, and its most lasting effect was in the inspiration men carried back to their parishes. A mimeographed paper, *Urban Africa*, was started in April 1963 to keep such men in touch with developments in thinking and experience. A further consulta-tion was held at Mbale in Uganda at the time of the Kampala conference of 1963.

Workshops on the urban problem have been held on a regional basis, such as that for East Africa at Dar-es-Salaam in May 1964 and reported in *The Church Meets Life in the Town*. Against the background of its analysis of the problems of town-dwellers, the report is significant for its stress on the structure and pattern of the town congregations, whether thought of in relation to worship, witness or service. It is particularly concerned with the carrying over into the town of the essence of African rural community life. The Mbale conference recommended the importance of studying the 'missionary structure of the congregation': a study which is, in fact, being currently undertaken on a world basis through the World Council of Churches in Geneva under the direction of Dr Hans J. Margull. He brought the first fruit of this study to the Dar-es-Salaam conference. It may seem commonplace to state that 'the task of the Church in a modern urban society is to be shaped so that it will meet the urban man where he is'; yet to recognise this is itself a step forward. The emphasis is on flexibility. A Church able to meet urban man both in his home and at his place of work, where different moral standards pertain, cannot expect to effect the meeting in the person of its ordained parish ministry; it must do so through the laity, the people of God who make up the town congregation. This calls, at the home end, for house-church groups for Bible study relating the Bible to harsh daily problems, for local community worship, including the Eucharist, and, in the factory, for personal witness through the fellowship experienced there among workmates. The Dar-es-Salaam report therefore lays emphasis on the training of the congregation to fulfil its mission, as well as on lay participation in the conduct of worship, and on the need for close co-operation in pastoral concern between urban congregations and the rural congregations from which the town labour force is recruited.

A similar workshop for West Africa, held at Lagos in August 1965, has added significance in that, with two exceptions, all the lecturers were Nigerians, including university lecturers in geography, extra-mural studies and economics, a barrister, a psychiatrist, and a director of radio programmes. The two non-Nigerians were a Cameroonian theology lecturer and a United States professor of sociology seconded to the University of Lagos, and himself a Roman Catholic priest. Townsmen were present from Abidjan (Ivory Coast), Accra (Ghana), Aba (Nigeria), Conakry (Mali), Cotonou (Dahomey), Douala (Cameroon), Enugu (Nigeria), Lagos (Nigeria), Lomé (Togo), Port Harcourt (Nigeria), Porto Novo (Dahomey), Tema (Ghana) and Yaoundé (Cameroon). Up-country mining communities in Liberia and Sierra Leone were also represented. Well aware of the practical difficulties, the Church in Africa in its study organisations is wrestling with the important issue of urbanisation.

The problems of life in African towns are very closely related to the race problem, for it is in the towns that much of the antagonism between white and black is generated and kept at heat. In South-Central and Southern Africa, the critical issues raised for the Church by the racial pattern of society were considered in the consultation on Christian Practice and

Desirable Action in Social Change and Race Relations held at Mindolo in May 1964, to which reference has already been made. The Christian Council of South Africa, at its biennial meeting in Johannesburg the same month, discussed some of these issues in the context of mission.[19] The newly formed Christian Council of Rhodesia held an important consultation at Salisbury in August 1965. Its report, *The Church and Human Relations*, forms a penetrating and incisive judgement on the state of Rhodesian society a few months before the illegal declaration of independence.

Several of these national studies deal briefly with the relation of the Church to African custom. The most detailed study is a much earlier one, that by the Ghana Christian Council in 1955: *Christianity and African Culture*.

Finally, there have been several studies on the pattern of the ministry and its recruitment: *Training for the Ministry in East Africa*, by F. G. Welch, 1963; *Why Don't They Answer?*, consultation at Yaoundé in November 1963; *The Crisis in the Christian Ministry in Uganda*, conference at Makerere in May 1964; *The Crisis in the Christian Ministry in Kenya*, consultation at Limuru in September 1964; and the AACC paper, *The Crisis in the Christian Ministry in Africa*, 1964.

★

So we move from the all-Africa level nearer to the local congregations, and reach two possible centres for studies of these same topics: the theological colleges in which the ministry is trained and, fewer in numbers, lay training centres. In the former, a break-through has not yet been achieved. The curriculum is in most cases too much tied to a traditional Western pattern. Students can still come away from their lecture-room after studying the first two chapters of Mark's Gospel—with its account of the touch of Jesus of Nazareth on different kinds of illness, including mental sickness—without having come to grips either with the failure of their own Church, despite its hospitals and clinics, to exercise a full ministry of healing or with the success of some Independent Churches in this respect. There are, however, some tentative beginnings in changing the method of learning in theological colleges. The syllabus for the East African Diploma in Theology includes as one of its subjects 'The Work and Mission of the Church'. As an introductory textbook for this course, F. B. Welbourn has written *East African Christian* which, among others, relates the subjects of AACC consultations to the parish situation. There are three journals whose aim is to stimulate the thought of the clergy: on the Protestant side, *Flambeau* from Yaoundé and *Ministry* from Morija in Lesotho; and, on the Catholic side, *The African Ecclesiastical Review* from Masaka in Uganda. In addition, several of the departments of religious studies sponsor bulletins for the publication of local material: the *Sierra Leone Bulletin of Religion*, the *Ghana Bulletin of Theology*, *West African Religion*, Nsukka, *Dini na Mila* (Revealed Religion and Traditional Custom), Makerere.

Nearer to the congregations are those Church newspapers that are more than retailers of parish news and deal with current social and political news in the context of Christian views on society. Among those with a Protestant standpoint are: *Target* (Kenya and Tanzania); *New Day* (Uganda); *La Semaine Camerounaise* (Cameroon). Roman Catholic periodicals of this calibre include: *Kiongozi* (Tanzania); *Afrique Nouvelle* (Senegal); *The Independent* (Nigeria); *Afrique Chrétienne* (Congo-Kinshasa).

Training for the Protestant ministry is now usually on a united basis. There are United Theological Colleges in most parts of Africa: Trinity near Legon in Ghana; Trinity at Umuahia in Eastern Nigeria; Immanuel at Ibadan in Western Nigeria, and the Theological College of Northern Nigeria at

Bukuru; the Faculté at Yaoundé in the Cameroon; St Paul's at Limuru in Kenya; Kimpese College in Congo-Kinshasa; the Federal Seminary at Alice in South Africa. Several of these include Anglicans, Presbyterians and Methodists; at least one has more than twenty-five years' experience. Some of these colleges have recently been rehoused in new buildings, thanks to generous grants from the Theological Education Fund: an imaginative scheme inaugurated by the International Missionary Council, now the Division of World Mission and Evangelism of the World Council of Churches. Founded in 1957 with a grant of $2 million from the Rockefeller Foundation, to which the Mission Boards in North America added a further $2 million, the Fund has promoted theological education in Asia, Latin America and Africa. African colleges have received £342,000 in capital grants and £47,500 in library grants. Assistance has also been given to the surveys listed above on page 106 and to the Independent Churches in Africa for the training of their pastors. In addition, twelve regional staff institutes have been arranged by the Fund in which theological college staffs have shared their thinking on the shape of the curriculum of their colleges. It is to these staff institutes, as to the consultation of African theologians in Ibadan in January 1966, that African Christianity looks for the necessary impetus for change in the curriculum of ministerial training.

6

The Practical Response

THERE HAS been, then, no lack of conference and consultation. What of the practice? We take first some examples of the Church in its service to the community. Through lay training centres, the Church not only provides for the training of its members in the understanding and application of their faith, but offers training on an open basis for service to the community.

The Nyegezi Social Training Centre at Mwanza in Tanzania offers such service in the name of the Roman Catholic Church. Its courses are open to those of any race or religion in East and Central Africa, and are aimed at 'helping to train men and women who will contribute their time and talents to the building up of the nations in developing Africa'. There are two main courses of eighteen months' duration: social development, which includes community development, social ethics, cooperatives, adult literacy; and publicity media, which includes journalism, visual aids, photography. Entry qualification is a minimum of twelve years' schooling, preferably with experience in some employment. Houses are provided for married students, and a third course in community development is offered to those wives whose previous education does not qualify them for enrolment in either of the main courses. The White Fathers who are responsible for Nyegezi offer similar training for francophone countries at Bobo Dioulasso in Upper Volta and at Bukavu in Congo.

The Mindolo Ecumenical Foundation at Kitwe in Zambia has already been mentioned as the meeting place for a number of Protestant conferences. Its substantive purpose is training for development through courses in national development, youth leader training, community development, agricultural training and women's home training. Its national development short courses vary in length according to the time different groups can spare: two or three weeks for trade union officials or management trainees; the inside of a week for top-level management and union together; one day a week for self-employed shopkeepers whose need is in costing, accountancy and income tax returns as well as in the discussion of human relations. In 1966, Mindolo acted as host for a series of three-week courses run by one of the banks for its young employees, bank staff providing the teaching in banking techniques and the Ecumenical Foundation that in general background, including social and commercial ethics. A six months' course in home-craft and community service is available for married women, who bring their younger children with them. Associated with the Ecumenical Foundation, and sharing its residential facilities, are the Writing and Art schools of the Africa Literature Centre, founded in July 1959. Four to six months' courses in writing and journalism and fifteen months' courses in commercial art and book illustration are available equally to those who will enter Church or secular employment. At a recent course for literacy workers, four literacy assistants were being trained for service with the Zambia government. In both these centres, the fees are subsidised from Church sources outside Africa to make their service readily available to the community.

One of the more comprehensive services in this field is the

nine months' course in civics run in London by the Society of Jesus. Thirty students are enrolled each year from all parts of Africa. The course is designed to provide leadership training to enable students, on their return home, to contribute as much as they can to the development of their countries. Among the subjects studied are: social ethics, book-keeping, moral philosophy, political theory, social economics, credit unions and co-operatives, the meaning of Christianity. There are two requirements for enrolment: ability to follow lectures easily in English, and the beginnings, at least, of the kind of generosity that leads a man to sacrifice much for the sake of his country.

A hopeful feature of the gradually increasing number of Christian lay training centres is the lack of uniformity in their curriculum. They are all experimenting, those mentioned above and such new foundations as the Anglican-Presbyterian Centre at Chilema in Malawi, the Nigerian Christian Council Centre for the Study of Church and Society at Ibadan, and the Edendale Lay Ecumenical Centre in Natal.

Alongside a main market and forming the junction between two rapidly expanding townships of Luluabourg in Kasai province, Congo, is a plot of about three acres which the Presbyterian Church has obtained for the young people of the townships. Temporary buildings provide for reading room and lending library, table games (the temporary beginnings show that three times the accommodation must be provided for table tennis in the permanent buildings than the original plans had allowed), a room for debates and films, and classrooms for typewriting, sewing, music, French, English and Bible study. Membership is by subscription—nominal related to overheads, real in relation to wage levels of young workers or pocket money of older secondary school pupils. The first permanent erection was a surrounding wall. With 500 members, in the late afternoon between 300 and 400 stream in to play or watch football and volley ball. A swimming bath and running track are planned, and an ultimate membership of 1,000. Two full-time wardens, Congolese and American, with a Peace Corps typing instructor, are assisted by volunteers in a down-to-earth programme which is responsive to the expressed needs of the members. Capital and partial recurrent funds come from overseas, but the local Presbyterian Church congregation is actively involved through the servicing of the club.

In Kenya, the Mau Mau rebellion not only brought to light the problems of the villages but also those of the Nairobi townships, with their increasing population of dead-end primary school leavers. One result was the opening of community centres associated with the different Churches. Another was the Christian Industrial Training Centre at Pumwani, where 144 boys follow a two-year post-primary course in carpentry, fitting, blacksmithing, motor mechanics, electrical fitting or radio repairs. Half the instructors are Kenyans, the remainder are recruited through overseas Churches. So successful has been the placing of students and so great the need that a similar training school is now being opened in Mombasa for 200 boys. Both these centres are run in the name of all the Protestant Churches through the Kenya Christian Council. An educational service of a very different kind, under the Christian Churches' Educational Association in Kenya, is the school at Mombasa for the physically handicapped. The pupils, of normal intelligence, have been physically affected by polio, cerebral palsy or some other crippling disease, and the school environment is adapted to their special needs.

For the past five years, a nurse has lived in the small town of Imesi in Western Nigeria, some 25 miles from her base hospital at Ilesha. In an investigation into the protein deficiency disease of young African children, *kwashiorkor*, she has kept records of every baby born in the village during this period and of its later welfare. The Church hospital, in conjunction with the World Health Organisation of the United Nations and with the whole-hearted co-operation of the village mothers, is thus contributing to the fuller knowledge of this serious condition of children. Far removed in scale as well as distance is the Kilimanjaro Christian Medical Centre now being built at Moshi in Northern Tanzania to provide training for doctors and paramedical workers. Drawing on resources in finance and personnel from Lutheran Churches and overseas government aid through the Lutheran World Federation, the Centre will lack nothing in terms of an up-to-date teaching hospital. Between this £1·5 million project in Tanzania and the nurse living in a village house in Nigeria lies a range of medical services offered in the name of Christ, always a blending of the best available medical skill with that love and care for the patient which the Healer of Nazareth inspires.

In leprosy, control and treatment have just reached a new and rather unexpected stage. Recent drugs seemed so certain to cure that governments throughout the world have been putting all their resources into large-scale outpatient treatment to the exclusion of hospitalisation, only to find that the number of leprosy patients is not decreasing. It now seems that many who have begun to receive treatment have desisted before full cure was achieved on finding during the long course of the treatment that some of the ancillary defects of leprosy, deformed hands and feet or disfigured features, still occurred. Christian hospitals in the meantime had been concentrating their care and attention on just these needs: sandals to prevent secondary infection of foot lesions, remedial exercises and handicraft training, foot and skin surgery. In this they were only able to serve the few. With the recognition that much of this remedial work, if begun early enough, can be carried out by paramedical workers after comparatively short courses of specialised training, a new strategy is emerging. This is to carry out together mass medical and mass remedial treatment, with central hospital bases for any necessary surgery. The International

[113]

Society for the Rehabilitation of the Disabled has taken the initiative in planning a training centre for these workers at Addis Ababa, the All-Africa Leprosy and Rehabilitation Training Centre. As most of the advances in rehabilitation techniques in surgery, physiotherapy and leprosy social work have occurred at Christian institutions, it is the existing Christian hospitals that are being asked to second the necessary experienced staff. This is the latest page in the story of the service of such societies as the American Leprosy Mission and the Leprosy Mission of London (formerly the Mission to Lepers).

There are nearly 750,000 reported refugees in Africa. Many more are not listed, for they have crossed national but not tribal boundaries and found unannounced refuge within their own tribal organisation. Half of the total are from Angola, Mozambique and Portuguese Guinea and are in Congo, Tanzania and Senegal respectively. Over 100,000 from Rwanda are in Burundi, Uganda, Congo or Tanzania. Many from the Southern Sudan are in Uganda, Congo or the Central African Republic. All these are mainly village people in family groups, and part of local mass migrations. The smaller numbers from South Africa and Rhodesia, on the contrary, are usually townsfolk with return doors barred against them by name. African governments have been very generous to refugees in allotting farmland and opening up to the children opportunities in an educational system which does not yet meet all the needs of their own citizens. Rehabilitation—medical, social and economic—is a shared task amongst governments, the United Nations' High Commissioner for Refugees, and the voluntary agencies. These latter include the Churches in both a fund-providing and servicing capacity, and other fund-providers such as OXFAM, European trade unions, War on Want.

The two major arms of international Christian service for refugees are the Catholic Relief Agency and the Division of Inter-Church Aid, Refugee and World Service of the World

Council of Churches. These two Church organisations handle, not only the funds raised by overseas Churches, but also large quantities of gifts in kind, of which by far the largest source is the Commodity Distribution Program of the United States government. Under the provisions of Public Law 480, agricultural produce bought in by the government under home market price guarantee is made available free to areas of short supply overseas, and the United States meets the cost of ocean freight.

The pattern of working in the Congo is typical of other countries. There the special relief agency of the Protestant Churches, a subdivision of the Congo Protestant Council known as the Congo Protestant Relief Agency (CPRA), is manned by administrators specially appointed from Europe or America with Congolese assistants and, at the point of personal contact with Angolan refugees, with the help of missionaries formerly stationed in Angola. A visit to the main point of reception in the Lower Congo in 1966 was a reminder of the continuing nature of the task. In the first six weeks of the year, some 3,000 new arrivals from Angolan territory had been registered; many of them required periods of hospitalisation because of exhaustion or wounds, and all needed food rations for several months until they could reap a first harvest from the land allotted them. The monies and goods handled by the CPRA form a considerable enterprise. In 1965, the Agency handled about £800,000 in cash for refugees (Angolan, Rwandan and Sudanese) and also for social service projects related to Congo itself. In the same year, it distributed materials, mostly US government foods and privately donated medicines and clothing, to the value of about £700,000. The CPRA makes a special contribution to the serious shortfall in medical personnel through 'Operation Doctor', a scheme by which expatriate doctors give short terms of service, from six months to two years, to fill emergency vacancies in mission and government hospitals. In the first three years of its working, over sixty offers of service were accepted.

In Tanzania, the Tanzania Christian Refugee Service is a contribution of the Lutheran World Federation on behalf of all the Churches. In co-operation with the government and the United Nations, it has already carried out extensive resettlement programmes for Rwandan refugees. An encouraging indication of integration is that some of the first refugees to complete a teacher-training course are being posted to schools away from the area of the refugee villages. A further scheme is helping 10,000 Mozambique refugees to find permanent resettlement. The member Churches of the Tanzania Christian Council are involved in helping the Christian community among the refugees to become fully part of the Christian life and witness of the country. An observer with experience of refugee work in Europe after the Second World War has commented that refugee work in Africa today is more 'indigenous' than it was in Europe. Fewer international experts are being sent in from outside; much more is being achieved through local workers.

The more general work of the Churches' service agencies may be illustrated from the launching in 1964 by the World Council of Churches, through its Division of Inter-Church Aid, of a $10 million fund to meet emergency situations in Africa. Subsequently, a survey of a number of countries was undertaken by Lord Caradon (then Sir Hugh Foot) and Dr Z. K. Matthews, and these priorities were drawn up: refugees; youth; rural development and agriculture; urban problems; teacher training; secondary and higher education; special projects relating to women and society. A special agency has been set up as part of the All-Africa Conference of Churches to administer the fund, and in particular to examine and approve projects seeking assistance. The board responsible for directing this agency consists of a Nigerian, a Zambian, two Ghanaians and a Cameroonian. Among the projects already being aided by this Ecumenical Programme for Emergency Action in Africa are:

Rwandan, Mozambiquean and South African refugees; the Kenya Christian Council Institute for the Training of Youth Leaders; a Congo agricultural training scheme; and buildings for the expansion of certain Zambian secondary schools.

Over the last few years, at the request of the World Council of Churches and the Vatican, a study has been undertaken jointly by the Federation of Socio-Religious Research Institutes (FERES) based at Louvain and the Institute of Social Studies (ISS) at The Hague. This study, financed with a grant from the Ford Foundation, encompasses an inventory of institutions and activities by Churches and Church-related bodies in the fields of education, health and social action, in Asia, Africa and Latin America. In addition, six field studies are under way, of which two are in Africa: the role of Church-related primary education in Tanzania, and the role of medical personnel, both 'Western' and 'traditional', in Cameroon. The inventory and the field studies will be published in 1967 and 1968 respectively.

★

It can rightly be pointed out that in most of these service institutions, just as with aid on the governmental level, the major contributions in finance and personnel come from the Church outside Africa and not from indigenous Christians. This is true, yet local participation—in personal service, in responsible administration, and in personal giving—is increasing fast. We could pick at random from among the names of great African headmasters and principals of Church secondary schools and teacher-training colleges, or refer to the editor and staff of *New Day* in Uganda, to the head of the Church blind school in Northern Ghana, and to women demonstrators in home economics programmes. We take just a few examples.

Christians round Dabou in the Ivory Coast have for long

desired to express their faith through medical service and have repeatedly requested outside help for this. At last a hospital was planned to serve as the centre of a rural medical service. Youth clubs and other youth groups in the Methodist Church in Britain undertook to raise the £150,000 needed during the winter of 1964–5. From their membership came offers of service of an architect, a works' foreman, a bricklayer, a carpenter, an electrician and a plumber. When the Ivory Coast Church learned of the raising of the money and of these volunteers, they said that if young people in Britain could push hospital beds from London to Brighton to bring in £3,000, young people in the Ivory Coast must do something. Every week during the building of the hospital, a different town or village congregation has sent along thirty of its young men as building labourers, provided with their fares and food for the week by their congregation. By means of this voluntary labour the hospital will be opened in January 1967, barely two years after the raising of the funds.

Farmers in Northern Nigeria are served in their villages through a simply organised extension service run by the Evangelical Churches of Northern Nigeria and the Sudan United Mission. Through nearly forty part-time agents, themselves farmers, farming supplies are made available in the village at the least possible cost. As important as the low price is the fact that the supplies are obtainable on the spot after the farmers come home from work in the evening, rather than from a town store 50 or 100 miles away. Supplies include seeds and chicks, insecticides and seed dressings, ploughs and spare parts, chicken wire and mosquito screening, and domestic sprays. A revolving loan fund is maintained for the provision of stock to young farmers who have been to a central farm for short periods of training in mixed farming. The agents receive a 5 per cent commission on sales; most of them give more than freely of their time in going out with farmers to their individual farms to pass on something of the little extra know-how that has come to them in the course of their time as 'Faith and Farm' agents.

In an area of similar farming, this time in Northern Ghana, the Roman Catholic Church has provided the stimulus for the setting up of Credit Unions; that round Jirapa, for example, having steadily built up substantial reserves.

There are two possible policies in agricultural development, to be regarded as complementary: taking village farmers where they are and by improvements rather than by radical change in method seeking to improve their output; and taking school-leavers and introducing them to mechanised farming. Two examples of the latter method are the White Fathers' training centre at Damongo in Ghana, and the Mindolo course in Zambia. At Damongo, training is given in the use of tractors and auxiliary machinery; each farmer is set up with a tractor and basic tools while more expensive machinery, such as a maize harvester, is available on a hire basis. In both these schemes, pupils have to be placed in new settlements and cannot return to a communal strip of land in their village. An example of the gradual method is the Catholic centre at Bam in Upper Volta. It is not an agricultural research station; it is a centre where village catechists can experience through demonstration and practical involvement proved ways of increasing crop yields and such new methods as the replacing of mattocks by animal-drawn ploughs and the use of simple irrigation to maintain a regular supply of green vegetables. Thus, when they are back in their villages they are equipped to be 'animators': those who form the spearhead of support for the government agricultural demonstrator, keeping the issue alive when he has gone on to another area, with a sense of responsibility for encouraging any who flag in following out the new methods.

In February 1966, the Christian Rural Fellowship of Nigeria and the Institute of Church and Society of the Nigeria Christian Council, with help from Agricultural Missions, New York, held a consultation at Zaria for rural and agricultural workers from West and Central Africa.[1] Their conclusions pointed in the same direction: that the Church should only occasionally be concerned with large-scale agricultural schemes; rather it should be providing in every village a few men and women who can give a lead in inspiring community action in village life—to be, in the French phrase, 'animateurs ruraux'.

If an inventory could be made, it would be found that service offered through specific Church institutions, as in the examples given so far in this chapter, is but a small part of the whole. The greater part lies below the surface, that given by individual Christians in their daily work and leisure time. We recall the many senior officials in government welfare departments who graduated to their present work through teaching after training in Church colleges, and the African international civil servants in UNESCO, WHO, FAO and the Economic Commission. We think of the members of the board of management of the Blaize Memorial Institute in Nigeria, or of the retired minister who runs the only children's home for African children in Rhodesia. He started the work during years spent on a country station, when he took into his own home half a dozen, then up to a dozen, boys in need of care, off the streets of Salisbury. Today in buildings on the outskirts of Salisbury he cares for fifty-six boys and girls. He and the others we have mentioned would be embarrassed by this publicity of their work. They would all, however, say that the motive in their service was that they had been brought into touch with Jesus Christ, and not that they happened by nature to be among the less thoughtless of citizens.

It is as we touch the springs of that selfless service which is truly unconscious that the service and witness of the Church are seen to be one. For the Christian, service stands in its own right as part of human compassion; it is at the same time part of his witness, for service and witness are one. God may use loving service to kindle hope and faith, but the act of service itself is a spontaneous outreach of love. The Christian knows that, for himself, the many pulls towards self-centredness have not been loosened by his own effort but by the grace of God in Jesus Christ. Where it is possible to offer service through a Christian community as such, this experience will not be deliberately hidden out of a concern lest service be interpreted as proselytising. The morning worship of such a Christian community is open for others freely to share at their will, whether it be in the hospital chapel at Kilimanjaro or the Centre chapel at Mindolo. The love which finds expression in the many acts and attitudes which the commerce of each day's life affords, also seeks expression in words so that the Word made flesh may receive the conscious recognition that is His due. The obverse of service is witness.

★

During the past seven years the town of Port Harcourt in Eastern Nigeria has been transformed from being merely a terminal port into a centre of industry. The change has been brought about by oil, not the palm oil of the old 'oil rivers' but the natural oil and gas welling up through bore-holes to be exported as crude oil, refined at Port Harcourt for Nigerian and West African use or, as gas, to provide power for new industrial estates. To the port's own multiplying population is now added the influx of village youth. Port Harcourt is the magnet, but employment lags. Neither oil companies nor industry can compete in the world market without the maximum of automation; the oil refinery, representing capital investment of £12 million, gives employment to 160 men. So this rapidly growing nexus of built-up areas separated by arms of the creek presents a complex of problems: a dangerous juxtaposition of 'haves' and 'have-nots'; bad housing; unemployment; labour–management clashes where senior management is expatriate and where rade unions have little experience in the art of negotiation.

In this situation, the Churches, for long established in the old town, found themselves out of touch with the community and its needs. The local Christian Council, under the chairmanship of the Anglican bishop, H. A. I. Afonya, and acting on the report of a visiting industrial chaplain from Britain, instituted what has come to be known as the Port Harcourt Project. This is an enterprise in which the resources of all the Protestant Churches are brought together in a common mission. In the name of all, individual workers seconded from different Churches serve the port chaplaincy, the social service, the industrial chaplaincy, the pastoral care of the expatriate community. The industrial chaplaincy is a two-man team, Nigerian lay and European ordained; it seeks to promote better under-standing within industry through study courses for management and labour and in personal negotiation. It provides a neutral and unofficial meeting ground for both sides of industry. Nearly forty evening classes for workers are run each week, voluntary instructors coming from among expatriates and Nigerians. On the social side there is youth work, social case work, particularly in relation to juvenile delinquency, care of motherless babies, infant welfare clinics and homecraft courses. A Women's Trade School is training girls for new types of employment, canteen workers and managers, home helps, factory machinists, secretaries. A multiracial school meets the special need of children of expatriate workers and of Nigerians posted away from home. The team of full-time workers and their many voluntary assistants in these various enterprises know themselves part of an integrated whole, which cannot be neatly divided into Anglican or Methodist, Dutch or Nigerian, Service or Mission. Those who provided the drive for an all-day Saturday clean-up of the streets and rain-gutters of Diobu Township were worshipping the following morning in one or other of the Diobu churches. Here was a new healing of old divisions.

The Practical Response

This working together of the Churches, though in places still hesitant, is often in advance of Europe and America. United action in the training of ministers has already been noted. Only one major union of Churches has yet taken place in Africa, that between the Congregational, Presbyterian, Methodist and Evangelical Churches in Zambia, forming the United Church of Zambia. Nowhere yet have the differences in the doctrine of the ministry which relates to episcopal ordination been resolved; though the United Church of Nigeria, originally planned to be inaugurated in December 1965, will achieve this, for the present postponement is due to non-theological factors. At the local level, the latest example of unity is at Gaberones, the new capital of Botswana (formerly Bechuanaland). Congregationalists, Presbyterians and Methodists have formed one congregation which uses one church building with the Anglican congregation; at many levels the two congregations are in fact one.

United action between the Protestant and Roman Catholic Churches, except in such spheres as educational planning, is only very recent. National Christian Councils are Councils of Protestant Churches. The almost completely Anglican nature of the Protestant Church in Uganda and the consequent absence of any need for a Protestant Christian Council there in the past opened the way to the formation, in 1963, of the Uganda Joint Christian Council with two co-secretaries, Roman Catholic and Anglican. Founding members are the Roman Catholic and Anglican Churches of Uganda, but the door is left open for other Christian Churches to join later on a basis of accepting the Apostles' Creed and baptism by water in the Threefold Name. The aim is stated as: 'to achieve joint consultation with the object of coming to joint decisions for common action on matters of mutual interest'. There are three subcommittees for the fields of education, social services and communications. In the constitution of the newly formed

Christian Council of Lesotho (formerly Basutoland), hitherto
a subgroup of the Christian Council of South Africa
there is special provision for the Roman Catholic Church to be
an 'associate member': a more definite relationship than the
'observer' status in some other countries. In the service of
dedication for this new Council held in the Evangelical church
at Maseru, the sermon was preached by the Roman Catholic
archbishop, the Most Reverend Emmanuel Mabaothana.

An even more comprehensive Council is that formed in
March 1966 in the Gambia. The Christian Council of the
Gambia has as founding members the Roman Catholic,
Anglican and Methodist Churches. Membership is open to any
'Christian Church in the Gambia which worships one God in
the Trinity of the Father, Son and Holy Spirit, which accepts
the Scriptures of the Old and New Testaments, which has an
established organisation, which teaches its members the
Christian way of life and exercises Christian discipline, and
which is prepared to work in co-operation with the other
member Bodies'.

The Octave for Christian Unity in January has been observed
for several years in West Africa with services in which Catholics
and Protestants worship together, as in Abidjan and Kumasi.
In 1966, at Yaoundé, this took the form of a large open-air
meeting. In East Africa, also in 1966, there was joint Anglican
and Roman Catholic evensong in Swahili in the Catholic
cathedral at Mtwara at which the bishops of both Churches
gave short addresses on unity and pronounced the blessing
simultaneously. A regular feature for some years at Maseru in
Lesotho has been a day's study conference of some forty to fifty
people, ordained and lay, from all the Churches. In the planning and carrying out of these conferences, Evangelicals,
Catholics, Anglicans and Methodists have been undifferentiated
participants. At a recent meeting, under the chairmanship of a
Catholic Lesotho priest, papers were read in the morning on the

nature of the Church from the Catholic, Methodist and Reformed (French) viewpoints, and in the afternoon on African Music and Expression in Worship. At Yaoundé in Cameroon, such meetings are held on two levels: small private study groups of theologians to discuss such subjects as the Eucharist, and larger meetings, to which fifty or sixty people are invited, on such subjects as the Christian approach to Islam, African music and liturgy. More generally, informal consultation between scholars is widespread; for example, historians of both traditions serve on the committee of the Society for African Church History, which was inaugurated in Freetown, Sierra Leone, in 1962 and is now constituted on a continent-wide basis.

The Pan-African Catechetical Conference held at Katigondo, Uganda, in August 1964, had as its first resolution:

> Having in view the common love for Holy Scripture which unites all Christians, the needs of the ecumenical movement, and the absolute need for Scripture in the vernacular, the Pan-African Catechetical Conference earnestly requests the hierarchies in all African territories where deemed advisable, to contact the Protestant authorities in order to work together for the early publication of both the Old and the New Testaments in versions adequate both exegetically and linguistically.[2]

Bible translation or revision in several languages is now in the hands of committees drawn from both Protestants and Catholics. The Catholic bishops in East Africa have agreed with the British and Foreign Bible Society for the printing of an edition of the Bible in Union Swahili as prepared by Protestant translators which will contain the deutero-canonical books and selected notes and commentary from the Jerusalem Bible. At the same time, a new translation committee has been set up representing the Catholic bishops and the Christian Council of Tanzania to revise the existing Swahili text and to adapt the notes and commentary, so that an edition may be produced for use by all Christians.

The common use of school chapels is a growing practice. St Peter's chapel at Nyakasura School in Toro, Uganda, has been consecrated for Anglican and Catholic use. A chapel is being built at the Government School at Navrongo in Ghana where worship will be together in all but the sacraments, though there will be one common altar table. The plans for the Christian Centre at Dar-es-Salaam University have a single circular chapel, with two small circular oratories for pastoral consultation, one for Protestants who share a common chaplain appointed through the Tanzania Christian Council, and one for Catholics.

The university situation at Dar-es-Salaam is a reminder of the Churches' responsibility in the student world. In the last ten years thirty-two new universities have been opened in Africa. The present 60,000 students will have become 300,000 before 1980. The needs of this community, both students and professors, are not being met by the Church, and there is a growing gulf between Christian students and the Churches. The few chaplains are mostly expatriate. On the Protestant side there are differences of judgement as to method in fulfilling a ministry to students, depending in part, though not completely, on the type of residential campus in the different universities. But the greatest weakness of the Church in the universities lies in the polarisation of Protestants between what, in English-speaking terms, has unfortunately to be described as 'Student Christian Movement Christians' and 'Inter-Varsity Fellowship Christians'.* We say 'unfortunately' because this juxta-

---

* This polarisation is now expressed more generally in the Churches through the formation in 1966 of the Association of Evangelicals of Africa and Madagascar as distinct from the All-Africa Conference of Churches. Indeed, just as the old divisions between denominations transferred to Africa from the West are being broken down, a new division is being imposed by Christians from Europe and America, namely, that between the main Christian tradition and the exclusive evangelical groups.

position itself perpetuates the hardened concepts which each group too often attributes to the other, and makes the very use of the titles of these movements a stumbling block. It is understandable, therefore, that the Tanzania Student Christian Fellowship has deliberately decided to abstain from membership of either of the two world bodies, the World Student Christian Federation and the International Fellowship of Evangelical Students. In this, as in some of the secular 'either—ors' of today, Tanzania opts for non-alignment. Regrettably this cuts Tanzanian Christian students from much-needed fellowship with those in other African universities, where there are groups affiliated respectively with one or other of the world bodies.

An experienced observer, whose knowledge of student life in Africa is profound, has recently commented:

> This very hardening of these positions, often encouraged by expatriate university teachers, has led in many cases to both scm and the Christian Union becoming virtually 'closed societies' more intent on winning adherents to their position than on communicating the Christian faith in an attitude of love, humility, and openness to university teachers and students for whom Christian faith is often without meaning and therefore no longer a live option.

The most urgently needed contribution to Africa from the Church in the West is reconciliation at home between 'conservative evangelicals' and 'liberal ecumenicals' (wretchedly ugly names for followers of the carpenter of Nazareth): a reconciliation which accepts a man's allegiance to the Lord Jesus with simple gladness whatever be the road by which he has come to know his Lord. Then in African universities a Christian presence may become more manifest.

Within Africa the historic Churches are beginning to enter into fellowship with the Independent Churches, a few of which have applied for membership of the Christian Councils. The

Interdenominational African Ministers' Association of South Africa includes quite a number of Independent Church pastors. Some of the larger Independent African Churches in South Africa have now formed the African Independent Churches' Association. At the conference at Queenstown in 1965 which made this decision were fifty leaders representing forty-five Churches. A year later about 150 more Churches had applied for membership. The basis of membership is: 'The Association is based upon the Word of God, upon belief in God the Father, Jesus Christ the Son, Redeemer and Lord, and in the Holy Spirit.' It is not without significance that the constitution contains a clause to the effect that if at any time the Association is dissolved, any monies standing to its credit would be automatically transferred to the Theological Education Fund as part payment for the assistance given by that Fund to the African Independent Churches of South Africa. A liaison committee formed of representatives of the South African Christian Council, the Interdenominational African Ministers' Association and the Christian Institute of South Africa is seeking ways of assisting the new Association in the training of the pastors of its member Churches. An existing Bible correspondence school has been asked to extend its work with overseas aid so as to offer a recognised course in biblical and theological study to the members of the Association. In addition, discussions are proceeding with the theological college at Evaton in the Transvaal of the African Methodist Episcopal Church so that a new course may be made available there for pastors who do not meet the existing post-Standard Eight entrance requirements. In Rhodesia, a retired Church leader has been active in arranging refresher courses for Independent Church pastors.

Opportunities for mutual understanding with Muslims are being sought in many areas. Catholic and Muslim leaders in Cameroon have drawn up a syllabus for ethical instruction in State schools, in which illustrations and scriptural references are taken from both the Koran and the Bible. The Muslim–Christian fellowship at Makerere in Uganda has held joint seminars on common theological problems such as 'suffering' and 'revelation'. Bishop Huddleston's mission to the University was supported by Muslims, and Christians have attended a series of Muslim lectures. These are steps, not to syncretism, but to greater understanding, which have to be offered in trust and confidence to God for Him to use in His way and His time.

★

These notes on activities of the Church all leave a haunting question: is the African Church of today really missionary? Are the passion and sacrifice which have been marks of the preaching of the Gospel from Saint Paul onwards part of the experience of this Church also?

Individual names come to mind. There is the university lecturer in West Africa whose Bible class in his home brings in the neighbours, members of his own and other Churches and of no Church; who is always ready to attend the eight-day naming ceremony of a neighbour's child and to say a simple Christian prayer which takes up the old into the new; who accepted the local party chairmanship and patiently sifted accusations of disloyalty to eliminate those which were a working out of old grudges. Or the civil servant who helped the ministers of his Church to recognise their pastoral responsibility for expatriates in their towns, and then, himself becoming an expatriate in Rome, by his personal witness increased the number of the worshipping community there. Witness is often expressed through quiet loyalty to the Church of Jesus Christ. At the memorial service to a West African judge whose last period on the bench was in East Africa, the story was told of a fellow-countryman calling on him there. A few years previously back home, this man, then a local party official, had been sentenced by the judge to a term of imprisonment for putting party law above state law. Now as ambassador at large, he made a special call at the judge's house and said: 'No regrets: we are grateful for the lesson you taught us.' The first Tuesday evening after the judge arrived in East Africa, an old friend called on him; after half an hour the host said: 'Excuse me, but I have to go to the choir practice.' The large crowd that attended the memorial service in that foreign town knew that these two parts of his life were a unity. Put alongside these the unschooled village woman, given the chance to learn to read in middle age, visiting a sick neighbour lying on her mat in the patio and reading to her of events in Galilee as if they happened yesterday.

Among the full-time servants of the Church there has been a willingness to go forth to strange places, successors of the Sierra Leonian ministers in the last century who served in Nigeria and Senegal and as far away as the lower Tana in Kenya. A Dahomeyan minister and his wife look across Ghana to a tiny grave in a village in the Ivory Coast, the price of their service to another country. Several ministers from Ghana and Nigeria have served recently in Gambia. One of them had just been accepted for a degree course at the university when the appeal from Gambia was made in his Synod; he and his wife had no children and could go more easily than some others; the university place was declined. During his service abroad the sincerity of this minister's faith rather than the power of any argument led a young Muslim to Christ. Angolan Christians have regularly sent one of their ministers at their expense to work in San Tomé. Across in the East, priests and catechists of the Anglican Church in Uganda have an honourable record of service in the Sudan and Rwanda.

Recently, the Evangelical Church of the Cameroon has inspired a decision of those Churches in Africa and the Pacific born of the work of the Paris Evangelical Missionary Society to join together in a mission to unevangelised areas of West Africa. They asked the Paris Society to be the medium for a new mission of international teams supported by all the Churches. The vision goes beyond Africa: 'multiracial missionary teams would be formed, they could work in France and Switzerland as well as in Africa and the Pacific'. The Yaoundé consultation on 'The Evangelisation of West Africa Today' drew attention to several areas where little Christian witness has taken place; one of these is the Fon region of Dahomey lying nominally within the area touched by the Methodist Church. Discussions have taken place between the Evangelical and Reformed Churches in Gabon, Lesotho, Cameroon, Madagascar and Zambia, the Paris Mission, the Methodist Church in Dahomey and the Methodist Missionary Society in London, as a result of which the first of the new teams, including evangelist, medical worker, agricultural worker and social worker, will go into Fon country under the auspices of the Methodist Church. Here are Christians, from Africa and Europe, willing simply to serve and not necessarily to perpetuate the particular tradition to which they owe their own nurture in the Christian faith. Here are African Churches prepared to meet the cost of such an enterprise.

The Protestant Churches of Northern Nigeria have been together involved since 1964 in a movement calling on every Christian to become a conscious witness. The 'New Life for All' movement has been based on local prayer groups, and supported by leaflets which Church members could use to start conversations with their neighbours. In providing the literature, the Scripture Gift Mission has been a helpful auxiliary. Non-Christians have been startled to find that those congregations were not closed-shops, and that they too were welcomed. Enthusiasm has in some places conflicted with an understanding approach to Muslims; in other places their respect has been won through acts of communal service, cleaning village streets and chopping firewood.

[131]

The message of the Church reaches town and village today across the air. National broadcasting systems make time available to the Churches for services and talks. The use made of this time is being enhanced through training courses and the setting up of recording studios. In addition, there are Christian broadcasting stations—such as ELWA in Liberia and ETLF, the Radio Voice of the Gospel, at Addis Ababa. The Lutheran World Federation owns the latter station and shares time for the Near East with the Near East Christian Council and for Africa with the All-Africa Conference of Churches. Recording stations have been set up in the major language areas so that programmes can be made locally and the tapes sent to Addis Ababa for transmitting. Transmissions are made in the following languages: Swahili, Nyanja, Malagasy, Zulu, Sesotho, Afrikaans, English and Hausa. The programmes are 70 per cent cultural and recreational, 30 per cent religious. At Addis Ababa there is a news room with announcers in English, French, Swahili and Arabic: a monitored news service provides an objective daily news session, more objective in many cases than that available locally. In a remote part of Central Tanzania, every evening fifty or sixty people come together to the one radio set in the village, to hear from Addis Ababa the Swahili programme recorded some weeks before in the studio at Moshi together with the live Swahili news bulletin. Linked with the specifically religious programmes are Bible Study correspondence courses, the applications for which give some indication of the very wide listener coverage. On the other side of the continent, ELWA in Liberia in addition to its religious and news programmes has a counselling department which answers correspondence from many parts of Africa.

7

The Response in Areas of Conflict

THE FIRES that are sweeping through Africa have not left the Church untouched. Men and women have died because they were Christians. Others have been ostracised by the community or imprisoned by the State because of their faith. The fellowship of the Church itself has been torn and sorely pressed. In so far as it was part of the very texture of the colonial period, bound up with the old conservatism yet begetter of the new radicalism, the Church has experienced the tension of change acutely within itself. The cost of too close conformation with older governments is a warning against becoming wholly conformed to the new. A price has been paid in standing for justice and mercy. Criticism of the State has been branded as disloyalty.

This is no new experience for Christians. In the days of the Roman Empire they found it necessary to defend themselves against the charge of being disloyal. Their apologists rejected the charge, claiming rather that Christians made the best citizens. 'They obey the established laws, but in their own lives they surpass the laws.'[1] 'Every man places in our treasury a small gift on one day in each month. These are disbursed for feeding and burying the poor, for boys and girls without

money and without parents, and for old men now house-
ridden, for the shipwrecked also, and for any in the mines, or in
the islands, or in prisons.'[2] They confidently appealed to the
emperor to consider 'our life, our loyalty and obedience to you
and your house'.[3] Yet what proved disconcerting to Roman
officials who recognised the truth in this claim was a stubborn
scruple in some Christians which prevented their complete
submission to the imperial sovereignty. 'Pity your old age', the
proconsul said to Polycarp, bishop of Smyrna; 'you have only
to swear by the genius of Caesar and I release you; revile the
Christ.' The old man preferred to accept death. 'Eighty and six
years have I served him and he never did me any wrong.
How then can I blaspheme my King who saved me?'[4]

In the tension arising from the desire to serve the nation and
all within it, yet never to surrender to it the final authority
which belongs to God alone, lies the strength of the Church's
witness in every continent, not least in Africa. In the pre-
independence years, however, the relation of missionaries to
the colonial governments meant that this tension was more
often academic within the theological classroom than active
outside it. Europeans had not personally know such tension in
acute form in their own country, unless they were among the
small minority who were pacifists by conviction. The concept
of law and order, with government policy changing gradually
and peacefully to meet the majority view of the electorate, was
a pattern of thought they carried with them into colonial
territories. Far-reaching criticism of government, tantamount
to a questioning of its right to govern, was in government eyes
sedition and in Church eyes un-Christian. Writing of the year
1957 in Zambia, Colin Morris refers to 'a staff meeting of the
Copperbelt Presbytery of the United Church of Central Africa
at which senior missionaries anxiously weighed the advisability
of accepting for the ministry a candidate who had been an
office bearer in Congress'.[5]

When the Gold Coast government ran its own newspaper for some weeks following the Accra riots of February 1948, in an attempt to 'steady the life of the nation', Church leaders responded with alacrity to the editor's request for a column to give a religious basis for an ordered society. To their surprise, many African colleagues refused to contribute. A fundamental difference of opinion was revealed as to who should be ordering the society. The day after the Governor's detention orders on Kwame Nkrumah, Dr Danquah and four other members of their party, the country woke up, literally overnight, to the conviction that it was time to have done with this foolishness of alien rule; from now on they would govern themselves. For Britain to have resisted this would have required not only an army of occupation but a denial of the philosophy which had steeled the British people to resist Nazi overlordship.

Because the tension up to this point had been between the Church and its missionary leaders, albeit largely hidden, and not a tension of existence between the Church and the State, the internal self-government and independence which followed February 1948 in quick succession found the Church in Ghana somewhat uncertain of itself. This was seen in hesitant views about ordained ministers as parliamentary candidates, about the requests of political parties for the setting aside of special Sundays for their local members to parade to church, about the national youth movement and Church youth movements. The Church faced the dilemma of appearing not to agree with the goals set before the nation when it questioned the means being employed. A new relationship with the State had to be thought through; in the process there were periods when there was no common statement of the Churches' position formulated. The real testing came when, in the years following 1960, the leaders of the national party sought to silence the independent voice of the Church by a policy of attrition. As the party leaders probed, points of resistance became evident. The principal of a Church teacher-training college firmly refused to allow a party cell any facilities differing from those that were available for any voluntary association of students within the corporate life of the college; a civil servant used every opportunity to question proposed legislation that consultation with his political chief provided. The heads of the Churches spoke firm words from the pulpit as they travelled the country. The only expatriate among them, Bishop Roseveare of the Anglican Church, was deported for several months; others, like the Catholic Archbishop Amissah, the Presbyterian Moderator Odjidja and the Methodist President Grant, risked the severer penalty of detention. More than once, a far-reaching government edict which violated the conscience of Christians was quietly amended, not because of any outcry in public but because of protests firmly voiced in interviews with high officials. Ordinary members of the Church also made their influence felt. This was consistently done through regular church attendance; the number of university graduates to be found in church on Sunday morning was significantly large. Individual men and women maintained their standards of work in public administration when leadership at the top was deteriorating. On a few occasions, public demonstration could prove effective, as when massed choirs of all the Churches sang through two whole days outside the prison in which a Catholic priest had been placed following arrest without trial. In the increasingly difficult days of the latter years of Dr Nkrumah's government, the Church was clearly one of the checks on its excesses.

Reference has already been made to the contribution of just one secondary school in Kenya to that country's first independent government. Before this came into being, the Church had passed through a more troubled period than that of pre-independent Ghana. The nationalist struggle of the early 1950s was motivated partly by conscious rebellion against

European domination, partly by a groping after the integrity of a people. It took form in ritual which cut across both tribal traditions and the Christian faith at the same time. Yet its appeal was to the deep roots of a people's loyalty. The excesses of the Mau Mau movement remain a warning of what can happen when a whole people continues to be humiliated and frustrated. At the time Christians, mainly in Kikuyu and Meru areas, faced a conflict of loyalties in which faith in Jesus Christ meant for many refusal to take the nationalist oath. 'The lips which have touched my Lord's cup at his table cannot touch this cup.' Some accepted death as an alternative to the oath, meeting it with a rare serenity. 'When you hear at midnight the knocking on the door then it is you know the power and peace of Jesus.' Some Christians joined the movement in the forest. Others, again, were caught between a nationalist movement to whose ritual they could not subscribe and the security campaign of a foreign government they could not accept; they suffered interrogation and imprisonment at the hands of the security forces. In the difficult years of reconciliation which followed, when wounds had to be healed in the community similar to those between collaborators and the resistance in post-war Europe, a factor in the healing was the strength and love released in Christians who had suffered for their conscience.

Other good came from the Kenyan tragedy. Christians of but a few years standing had been strengthened by the single-mindedness of the East African Revival Movement, the company of those who 'walked in the light'. This swing of the pendulum towards exclusive concern with personal salvation received a corrective in the sudden awareness of the conditions of life in the town communities, particularly in Nairobi. The Church's social conscience was aroused. The awakened sense of social justice found expression in the Christian Council camp for 'orphaned' children at Dagoretti, in the new community centres in the Nairobi townships, and in the trade schools for youths.

The solidarity of the Church over against the colonial government was nowhere more complete than in Malawi. The quotation from Colin Morris on page 134 continues: 'It is an indication of the revolution which has swept Central Africa over the past four years that many missionaries, especially in Nyasaland, have almost come to regard the churches in the African townships as branches of Congress or UNIP in Sunday dress.' A service in the open air in the Kanjedza detention camp near Blantyre in January 1960 confirmed this. Bibles were brought out and the text underlined in pencil. These political detainees were just a group of Church elders. They knew, too, that the missionaries working among them had for long expressed publicly what the Devlin Commission Report had recently stated: that the government was set on a collision course with African opinion. One Church of Scotland missionary, Tom Colvin, was now a prohibited immigrant. Another, Andrew Doig, had resigned from the Federal Assembly, where he had been a European member representing African interests, because the African Affairs Board set up to protect African interests in a majority white parliament was being effectively by-passed by the federal government. In Malawi, as in Ghana, the Church has had to rethink its responsibility within the State with the coming of independence. It causes no surprise that the most pertinent criticism of Dr Banda's policies comes from the same Church elders who spent the months of 1959 behind barbed wire; nor that, as in Ghana with Church leaders Amissah, Odjidja and Grant, such criticism achieves most when it is not high-lighted from outside.

The Church in the other northern part of the Central African Federation, Zambia, had a more difficult course than that of Malawi. There were more European members, particularly in the Copperbelt towns, and pastors and lay representatives tended to reflect their segregationist views in Church discussions. Even so, the balance was more truly held than it was south of the Zambesi. The Church in Zambia knew what Africans were thinking and represented it more adequately than did District Commissioners and European farmers. Men like Merfyn Temple for the rural areas and Colin Morris for the towns gave moral support to Kenneth Kaunda in days when the outlook was dark and the power of the Central Africa Party and the federal government seemed overwhelming. As with the despatches to the Church of Scotland from Nyasaland, so those to the LMS and the Methodist Missionary Society from Northern Rhodesia provided chapter and verse for a constant reminder to successive Colonial Secretaries in Whitehall that there was a formed opinion among the rank and file of Africans, including non-schooled country farmers, which resented white superiority expressed in the colour bar and most passionately demanded a say in the government of their country. Nor should John Moffatt be forgotten: farmer, civil servant and Christian layman, and the last great public figure in the long family line going back to Robert Moffatt and David Livingstone. He had striven from the inception of Federation to bring Europeans to accept an interpretation of partnership which many Africans at that time could have accepted, as in his Moffatt proposals adopted with only one dissentient in the Northern Rhodesia Legislature in July 1954, and, in somewhat different terms, overwhelmingly rejected in August 1955 in the Federal Assembly.[6]

A rather different pattern of the Church's life in time of crisis occurred in Rwanda. Here the revolt of a people was not directly against colonial rule but against minority tribal rule confirmed by the colonial power. In November 1959, before Belgium granted independence to Rwanda and Burundi, the older cultivating inhabitants of Rwanda, the Hutu, revolted against their pastoral overlords, the Tutsi. The Church had reflected the pattern of society. Thus, while its members were drawn from both peoples, the greater number of its leaders and

[139]

pastors were Tutsi. At the same time, there were bridges between the two communities within the life of the Church, and the ministrations of those Hutu who were qualified in the educational, medical and pastoral work of the Church were now readily accepted by Tutsi members. The 1959 rising led to many Tutsi becoming refugees in Burundi, Tanzania and Uganda, and to the setting up by the colonial government of camps for Tutsi refugees within Rwanda.

A Tutsi pastor, Yona Kanamuzeyi, served in one of these camp areas in the years following independence, winning the respect of Hutu officials as he helped in the integration of the older aristocratic community in the new nation. His was a ministry of reconciliation which earned the hatred of those on both sides who wished to perpetuate the old division. When, in 1963, an ill-advised and ill-fated attempt was made by refugees from outside Rwanda to reinstate Tutsi control, suspicion of complicity fell on the Tutsi community within the country. In the reprisals which ensued, Yona knew he was a marked man but he refused to leave his post for a more remote village. One evening he was taken from his home by soldiers and shot at a bridge where the invaders had fought with the national army. Two others taken with him by the soldiers were set free, his bearing in face of death having apparently shamed their captors. 'They were all amazed; they had never seen anyone go singing to his death, or walking, as he did, like a man just taking a stroll.' On being taken out of the army jeep at the bridge, he had asked permission to write in his diary. He wrote: 'We are going to heaven'; and then added, as completely as he could in the time, an account of his church's funds left in his house.[7]

In Congo, the darkest experiences of Christians in the years since independence have resulted from a similar tension to that in Rwanda: the position of the reconciler where passions have been aroused in a righteous cause and then got out of control.

But this was not to happen until independence was several years old. At first, the trials of the Church were those of adjustment. The mutiny of the Force Publique in protest against its Belgian officers early in July 1960 was an indication of the determination of the Congolese to be free of colonial control in every respect. It was the sign for the exodus from Congo of the majority of expatriates, whether government officials, traders, professional men or missionaries. The effect on a Church where self-government was further off than in many countries of the continent was catastrophic. There had, generally speaking, been much paternalism in the missions. Now Africans found themselves pitchforked into leadership, a situation to which they responded with fortitude and ability. It was a more fully African Church to which missionaries returned. But their return was not automatic, although in most parts of the country only a few weeks were sufficient to show that the outward trek had been unnecessarily precipitate. There was a questioning by Church leaders why most missionaries had acted under orders of their consuls like other nationals and left their charge at a moment's notice. They were prepared to welcome them back, but as individuals who were invited by the Congolese Church. There were variations in such a large country. In some areas, the new Church leaders themselves insisted that missionaries should come back only when the Church invited them. In others, the mission boards in America and Europe, accustomed to such procedure in other parts of the world, were now able to insist on this provision—sometimes against the judgement of Congo missionaries themselves.

So what had been a gradual process of devolution elsewhere happened overnight in many Congo Churches. This was the bright and positive side of the hurried evacuation. By the middle of 1961, many missionaries had returned, to adapt themselves to a new relationship and to throw themselves into the task of more rapid training of Congolese for leadership in education, medical service and the pastoral ministry. In this period, the history of the Church is the history of Congo: sharing in food shortages, in attenuated medical service, in the continuing political struggles; taking on very much the pattern of politics of the area. In a few towns, the presence of Ghanaian troops and Nigerian police—many of whom were Church members—brought for the first time a knowledge of the Church as not just partly American or British and partly Congolese, but as reaching into fellow-African countries.

It was the widespread rebellion against the central government in 1964 which was to bring persecution and death to many Congo Christians. The actions of the Simbas, or Lions, were usually unpredictable. They were often a group of un-disciplined troops, with many teenage hangers-on, under indifferent control. News of white mercenaries in action against them in any area led to reprisals against any white people in the neighbourhood, traders or missionaries. A number were killed, women were raped and men subjected to insult and humiliations. Among the Congolese it was Christians who suffered, for they were foremost in resisting the arbitrary acts of the Simbas and, in particular, in seeking to protect and hide missionaries. Whereas, in 1960, the African Christians had often shown indifference as to whether the missionaries stayed or left, now there was a great sense of care.

'Why did you shelter a white woman?' asked the Simba military court of one pastor. 'Because she is my sister in Christ, the child of my own Heavenly Father,' was the reply. Although he was condemned by the court to be shot, the effect of his bearing on the Simba major was such that he set him free. In another village the soldiers came to take a teacher whom they suspected of aiding a missionary. His wife persuaded him to go to a hiding-place in the forest while she faced the soldiers. She was taken away for questioning. In reply to one question it emerged that she and her husband had been married for twenty-six years and God had given them no children. The leader was so impressed by such fidelity that he gave her two soldiers to escort her home, saying, 'You Protestants, the way you talk you know how to put down the heart of a man whose heart is high with anger.' Despite orders against the holding of services, Sunday worship has been maintained. In one girls' school, a few Standard Six girls due to go on to secondary school have for over a year kept the school running and taught all the classes. During 1965 a midwife from a Church clinic delivered more than forty babies in hiding-places in the forest. Here is a Church which has come to maturity through trial.

South Africa does not offer the simple clear-cut choice of the village woman in Kenya or the pastor in Rwanda. More often the situation there calls for a deliberate, cold-blooded type of courage. Readiness to meet death at short notice may some- times be an easier decision than the calculated acceptance for one's family of ostracism from their own community, or for oneself of the solitary intimidation of ninety days' detention. Nor is the point of decision always clear. When allowance has been made for a majority of Church members, whose faith is not called in question but who are influenced more than they realise by personal ends and who are regrettably ill-instructed in Christian truth, there remain apparently valid choices which are in conflict. At the introduction of the Bantu Education Act some Christians felt it right not to hinder the government and agreed that Church school buildings should be leased for Bantu schools. Others, on principle, refused such co-operation. Among African and Coloured Christians, there are some who so despair of just treatment for their children and who fear for the warping of their personalities, that they question whether they should stop short of violence to change the existing order. They have friends in the Church who feel as strongly as themselves but whose interpretation of the faith rules out such an answer. There are many such points of tension in the South African

Church, within white congregations, within black congregations, within mixed Synods, between the Dutch Reformed Churches and the others.

With such tensions within itself, it has been difficult for the Church of Christ in South Africa to speak with a common mind. The bishops of the Anglican Church have spoken out on the injustice and inhumanity of apartheid, but in advance of the thinking and knowledge of the majority of their white members. So have the Roman Catholic hierarchy and the Christian Council of South Africa. The Methodist Church has greater lay participation in Church government and a larger proportion of African members—a statement by its Annual Conference is both more representative and more conservative than hierarchical epistles; but even so, when it has spoken on apartheid, it has been in advance of its white membership. In most of the white circuits, however, the African minister who recently held the annual office of President of the Conference (the Reverend S. Mokitimi) was made welcome. The heart of the Churches' weakness is that, although among white Christians there are many costly acts of help to Africans caught up in the viciousness of the system, behind bold statements of principle there lies a personal unwillingness to commit one's family to live with Africans as part of one common community.

It is here that the pastoral letter of the Catholic bishops of South Africa, dated July 26, 1966, is significant. Not only do they state:

> We find it necessary to reiterate that it is a grave violation of the dignity of the human person to prevent anyone, on grounds of race or nationality, from choosing his own mode of living, to restrict his choice of employment, his right of free movement, his place of residence, his free establishment of a family.

They also state what so few whites are prepared to accept, the rejection of the doctrine of 'separate but equal':

Man, by his very nature, must have the company of his fellow men. It is only through constant commerce with them, through brotherly dialogue, through the give and take of social routine, that his talents are sharpened, his personality developed, to fit him for his destiny both in time and eternity.

This social exchange knows of no impediment of colour, creed or class. On the contrary, where there are inequalities of education, economic condition, and the rest, close inter-communion becomes all the more necessary, and all the more fruitful.[8]

This is the very opposite of separate development. Here is a clarion call to Christians of all Churches in South Africa to put their weakness behind them, and to show courage. There are individuals among them who point the way.

Father Trevor Huddleston and Bishop Ambrose Reeves fought the Group Areas Act which took away from Africans their cherished freehold rights in Johannesburg. Professor Z. K. Matthews and Dr D. G. S. M'Timkulu resigned their university posts rather than continue to teach in controlled conditions inimical to the free expression of thought. Chief Luthuli chose to be deposed by the government rather than voluntarily to mute the voice of criticism. Archbishop Hurley and Bishop Inman speak out with a voice which the silence of many of their laymen cannot drown. And there are others. Here, a Dutch Reformed pastor faces the withdrawal of the invitation to serve his congregation, and with it the loss of home and livelihood, because he dares to associate himself with critics of the government's apartheid policy. There, a white woman risks the odium of her neighbours and the threat of restriction of movement because she does almost exactly that which Tertullian described in the year 197, disbursing funds for the relief of the dependents of those 'in the islands or in the prisons'. Or again, an

[145]

African pastor patiently seeks friendship with whites amid the criticism of fellow-Africans, expressing his faith in these words: 'My task is to build bridges, even when I can see the floods which will carry them away already bearing down on them.'

The Church in Rhodesia is that of South Africa in microcosm. The statement, *Human Relations in Rhodesia*, put out by a consultation of some ninety European and African Christians in August 1965, was far in advance of what the average white members of the Church are willing to accept in integration and equality of treatment for Africans. As elsewhere in Africa, the Church has provided the education through which Africans have graduated to take a place in society which their fellow-Christians now deny them. Joshua Nkomo and Josiah Chinamano, sent to vegetate in the detention camp at Gonakudzingwa in the hope that they will lose their desire to think independently, are Methodist local preachers. Ndabaningi Sithole in a similar camp at Gokwe is a Congregational minister whose book *African Nationalism* reveals something of the quality of these banished men.[9] Nathan Shamuyarira is another local preacher. His recent book shows time and again his desire to enter into a real partnership which the majority of white people in Rhodesia still refuse.

> Even the limited advances which were made never had the favourable impact they might have deserved among Africans because the decisions were taken for them, not by them or even with them. Paternalists never seem to understand that, if one is not party to a decision, one has no real obligation nor appreciation.[10]

And of the Church he says: 'The mainstream of Church opinion that determines policy is represented by those many Church leaders who accept the power structure in Rhodesia, and support it with all its inequalities; and the white congregations which support Ian Smith's segregation.'[11]

The Response in Areas of Conflict

There is now a big rift in the fellowship of the Church of Christ in Rhodesia. It is a rift between black and white, and between pastor and people. In white congregations, it is almost impossible for the white minister with a prophetic voice to exercise his pastoral ministry. In black congregations, it is equally difficult for the black minister with a word to speak about reconciliation between the races to exercise his. Loyalty to Christ conflicts with loyalty to 'Kith and Kin'; in this village, a black woman has her house burned down because she refuses to attend a political meeting in worship hours; in that suburb, a family is ostracised because they invite Africans to their home. Is this what Christ meant when He said that He came to bring not peace but a sword? The word most needed is that of the South African bishops. For, in Rhodesia as in South Africa, many European Church leaders, including 'liberal' ministers, do not subscribe to the paragraphs quoted above on 'social exchange' because in their hearts they know they are not ready to commit their families to its basic premise: letting people rub along together.

There remain two countries where the Church has suffered greatly in recent years: Sudan and Angola. In neither case can the full story yet be told. The disunity in the Sudan between the Muslim Arab north and the part-Animist, part-Christian, Negro south was a legacy of the new state from the colonial era. The south was restless under northern rule from the beginning and suspected that the policy of the government in Khartoum was integration in language and religion to the dominant northern culture. How far this was suspicion, how far fact, is uncertain. If it was only suspicion, it was never dissolved. There was increasing use of violence in the south by armed bands of southerners, with counter-violence by the army sent from the north to maintain order. In the fear of northern cultural domination and the reaction which accompanied it, southern Christians identified themselves with their community.

In February 1964, all missionaries were summarily expelled from the southern provinces. Then, in the summer of 1965, 'for reasons not satisfactorily explained, the army's fury was turned full upon the Christian Church in the south. Bishop Gwynne Theological College was sacked and burnt, as were many local churches. Pastors and congregations were scattered—many, including the two assistant bishops, becoming refugees in the neighbouring countries.'[12] Only one of the three senior southern Sudanese Roman Catholic clergy is still among his people in the south; of the others, one has been killed and one is a refugee. The Khartoum government has denied that its policy is aimed at Christians as such, but there are few signs at the time of writing to suggest that a basis for building up mutual trust has yet been found.*

In northern Angola, now sadly empty of some 400,000 of its population who have crossed into the Lower Congo, the Church suffered as part of the people, not as the Church. Organised revolt against the Portuguese government broke out in the north on March 15, 1961. It was accompanied by atrocities against individual Portuguese, of whom some 200 were killed. Far-reaching and indiscriminate reprisals followed in which thousands of Africans lost their lives. From this time, the trek into Congo from the northern area began, and still continues. Just as most of the people of the region are now in Congo, so is their Church. As villages have lost many of their

* In early December 1966, the Sudan government, responding to a request from the All-Africa Conference of Churches, invited a deputation to visit Khartoum and the three southern province headquarters, but not the outlying Christian centres. Sir Francis Ibiam (Nigeria, AACC president), the Reverend J. Gatu (Kenya), the Reverend Swailem Sidhom (Egypt) and Mr S. H. Amissah (Ghana, AACC general secretary) spent ten days in the Sudan. The suggestions they have made to the Sudan government to help it gain the confidence of southern exiles so that they will return home have not yet been made public Reports speak of friendly and outspoken discussions with government representatives, and of hopefulness among Sudanese Christians as a result of the visit.

leaders through shooting and bombing, so has the Church. Two factors on the other side of the balance sheet may be mentioned. The immediate response of the World Church to the needs of the refugees, so that they found help available as soon as they crossed the border, made a deep impression on them. Their realisation of the world-wide nature of Christian fellowship did much to strengthen them in their tribulation. They have also made their own contribution to the Congo Church, for they have filled the places on the farmland and in the village churches of the Lower Congo left vacant by the movement of Congo youths into the towns. In many of these villages, 10 per cent of the congregation are Congolese, 90 per cent Angolans.

In central Angola, however, men suffered because they were Christians. Concurrent with the steps taken to put down the rebellion in the north, action was taken by the Portuguese to eliminate potential African leaders elsewhere. Since the Protestant Churches had given responsibility in leadership to Africans to a greater degree than had the Catholic Church, this action became in fact directed mainly against Protestants. This was so marked that Christians began to hide their Bibles, since these were regarded by the soldiers as the mark of a Protestant. The full story of this annihilation of the cream of the educated young leadership of the Church and potentially of the Angolan nation can only in part be put together. It will make a grim story when it is fully told.

8

The Future

HERE then is the Christian Church, the One, Holy, Catholic and Apostolic Church, widespread throughout the continent in the form of many Churches. Its weakness is manifest; it faces the challenge of strong new movements of the mind and spirit. Has it had its day? Has it, so far as Africa is concerned, served its purpose in helping to cushion the change from 'feudal' to 'modern' forms of government and social organisation? Are the thinking and experiment and action outlined in the previous chapters merely a fumbling attempt to retain influence, to gain some new position of authority to compensate for privileges now being rapidly lost? Or has it a significant future? A secular historian will give his answer against the background of the rise and fall of civilisations and may well sum up against an institution which was born in the pre-scientific age and which clings so tenaciously to tradition. He will take note of all in the corporate life of the Church which reflects human selfishness and pride, and wherein the Church in Africa has clogged and not quickened the body politic. Yet he has also to reckon with those apparently spontaneous movements of history which throw carefully weighed judgements out of balance, whether they be the insistent winds of a Vatican Council or the quiet penetration of an East African Revival Movement. He must take account, too, of the personal testimony to their faith of schooled and unschooled alike, and of willingness to suffer rather than betray it.

The observer who accepts membership in the Christian Church as something God-given in his life—though he lives, like John of Patmos or Augustine of Hippo, in a time when the continued existence of the Church seems doubtful—and who recognises all its present weaknesses, may give a different answer. For him, the Church is the eternal fellowship in every generation within which men, created in the image of God, yet continually falling short of God's glory, are recreated by God's grace in the midst of this mortal life. The divided Churches, the one splintered Church, may become hardened as the institutional expression of this fellowship. It may happen with them, as with other human institutions, that it is better for them to have 'served their generation not without some glory than that they should outlive their age and power of service'.[1] If they resist recreation, then they will die; but a new expression of the one continuing fellowship will take their place. For one who throughout his life has found that this faith is a valid part of his experience and who knows that trust in God through Jesus Christ is the final answer to the need and aspiration of the human heart in its search for reality, for God, it is possible to believe that such faith can also fulfil African spirituality. He believes further that this faith can help African nations to achieve that ordering of society which tempers justice with mercy, and righteousness with the safeguarding of individual personality. He is not an easy optimist. The countries of Africa have difficult days ahead of them. These present years of turmoil in Congo can be seen as part of a long road to the wholesome well-being of a free people; but that cannot blind us to the sleeping sickness that is creeping back to areas from which it had been banished. The struggle for economic and national survival will be a hard one. As it grows more tense, it may become unpopular to be a member of a world society like the Christian Church. The children of today's nominal Christians may never come so near the Church as their parents. Large church buildings may meet the same fate as the Catholic cathedrals of the sixteenth and seventeenth centuries in the Lower Congo and Angola. Whether the Church in Africa is likely to continue to grow at the rate of the past fifty years, or become again a small minority movement or die out completely, each must assess for himself. There can be no definitive answer to the question which this survey set out to examine. But there have been hints during the course of this rapid review to suggest that here and there are roots which will not be easily cut off, and that the awareness of the presence of God in Jesus Christ in this man and that woman is a reality which they would be prepared to stake against life itself. We therefore believe that the Christian Church has still a contribution to make to the peoples of Africa, and that they have a contribution to make to the Church throughout the world.

Given this answer from within the Church, what shape of Church is seen? In principle, the answer will be the same whether the question is asked in America, China, Britain, Russia or Africa. Christians are to be leaven in society. Leaven loses its identity as it fulfils its work. The followers of Christ are to lose themselves, to be, like their Master, as the grain of wheat falling into the ground, losing its form that other grains may grow from it. This is not the picture of an institution. At the same time, there are no such beings as solitary Christians; they are part of a worshipping fellowship. The fellowship requires form, both for worship, the 'breaking of bread and prayers', and for the passing on of the faith to a new generation. The form must never become an end in itself; it only merits existence as it enables its members to be more fully themselves in the social life into which God has caused them to be born: of home, of work, of leisure, of the ordering of society. For it is in the give and take of life, since eternal values can only come in through the side door, never by careful striving, that they learn the lessons of eternity. Leaven or a separate identity? The lesson of the history of the Church is surely that, if circumstances force on Christians a deliberate choice, the greater danger lies in stressing the institution than in stressing a going out into society. He who seeks to save his life will lose it.

So we go back to the small town in Ghana from which we set out. Its people straddle the old and the new worlds. Some of its sons and daughters go out from it daily to their farms. They have brothers in Takoradi and Accra, London and Geneva. At the end of their days these will come back to a family house, and join the old men talking in the shade of a flamboyant tree. With this town we also keep in mind one other—Takoradi or Ndola, Bulawayo or Kinshasa—with its second generation of city-dwellers who have no roots in village or country town.

The Church there will not leave its mark on a new generation through the school or dispensary or demonstration farm, for these will be government activities. Any salt Christians can contribute to the wholesomeness of the community will be as they go as men and women from the Christian fellowship into the whole of life, its getting and its spending, its marrying and begetting, its organisation for security and freedom; going as farmers, policemen, lorry-drivers, teachers, mothers, carpenters, local government officials, politicians. In villages, members of the Christian fellowship will be found among those who are prepared voluntarily to contribute their time and patience to interpret government policy among their fellow-farmers, to be the 'animators' of the new agricultural society. In the same way, not because good qualities are limited to Christians, but because for Christians they spring from fellowship with Jesus

Christ, the nurse will take loving care into the hospital ward, the teacher a deep respect for personality into the classroom, and the sanitary officer integrity into his relations with contractors. Behind all of them will stand the local fellowship of Christians, the local Church. 'What we have seen and heard we declare to you, so that you and we together may share in a common life, that life which we share with the Father and His Son Jesus Christ.'[2] For this small fellowship has within itself a give and take of thought and personality and character through which men grow, the better to learn how to live together in the fuller fellowship of society.

Will they still be Romans, Methodists and Seraphims? The unity of 'all in one place' will increasingly be seen in a common name, though the fellowship of reading the Bible together and of praising God in the breaking of bread may be exercised within different groups even in a small town. This will be not so much because of dividing differences but because of human variety and numbers. Men need a place to feel at home.[3] Must there be one building, a church or cathedral, large enough to hold all members of the fellowship in that town at the same time? This may no longer be necessary; the visible unity of all can be expressed in Africa, when needful, in the open air, on the football ground or in processions. If there is a felt need for a great cathedral, it should surely be the result of the prayer and spontaneous giving of the people, not coming from donors across the seas or from money-raising pressures within the local community. If the leisure time and financial resources of too many members of the fellowship have to be devoted to the maintenance of the fabric of a meeting-place, albeit a place of worship, then the rhythm of worship in the fellowship and service in the community is thrown badly out of balance.

What is essential is that members of the fellowship can join in what has been the central act of the Christian Church through the ages: the breaking of bread and the pouring of wine—

symbols of a common purpose, sacraments of the forgiveness of
God that sets men free from guilt and shame. It is those who
eat of the bread and drink of the cup who form the local fellowship. It is this act of worship above all others that speeds men
and women on their way with an overflowing of love and
mercy. Who is to exercise the 'ministry of the Word and the
Sacraments'? Who is to break the bread? Must they wait in
each village and each township section until the full-time
ordained minister or priest can fit them into his crowded
itinerary? Both Protestants and Catholics recognise the need,
if there is to be an altar community in each locality, for the
farmer or carpenter or teacher to be entrusted with the representative responsibility for 'presiding' at the Lord's Table,
whatever be needed by way of ordination to effect this. And if
the carpenter, why not the mother? May not the hands which
bake the bread in the home, break it here in the family of the
Church? May not the reason behind the old taboos be turned
in a positive direction, and the one whose life-blood flows in
the new generation also be the minister on behalf of all? Be
this as it may, the Church in Africa cannot afford a professional
ministry on the Western pattern, any more than it can afford
the upkeep of mighty cathedrals. The full-time ministers it can
afford will be needed for different ministries: some, but not as
many as at present, for the parish; others for training lay
leaders; others again to serve different groups within society in
the study of their faith in relation to their profession; doctors,
teachers, politicians, technicians, managers, civil servants,
town-planners, farmers.

There will be those who claim the shelter of this Christian
community without entering its regular fellowship; these are
the 'lost' Christians of the censuses. God will touch their lives
at specific points, in the home, on the farm, at market, in the
factory. In the ritual of life each point can be a meeting with
the Creator and Redeemer: the eight-day naming of their

child* at home in which members of the Christian fellowship share; the harvest thanksgiving; a prayer in time of special need or danger. For these can all be given forms in the simple act or the easily remembered words which, being at the same time African and Christian, mediate God to men. Perhaps men will come less shyly to the breaking of bread when it can be done naturally; as when in a side-street in Mombasa the Lord's Table is laid in the eyes of passers-by in a shop-front used as a community centre so that they may see Christians participating in the simple act and, if Muslims, recognise that here is the Christian ritual.

To the Christian community, the local Church, is entrusted responsibility for passing on the faith to a new generation, through teaching and through introducing them to that challenge of Jesus Christ which may lead to personal committal. This is primarily a responsibility of the home, then of the Christian community as a whole. One of the oldest unchanged acts of religious ritual in the world is the Jewish Passover; enshrined in thought and experience from one generation to another because of its dramatic action and the father's response to the natural question of children: 'What are you doing that for, Daddy?'4 The acted catechism is more enduring than the written one. The centrality of the Christian faith is to be seen in the acts and accompanying words of baptism, marriage, committal in burial, of harvest thanksgiving, of the breaking of bread. Here lies the understanding use of those aspects of corporate worship which are didactic. So the form of the Te Deum translated from Latin into English into Fante, dating back to that day in the fourth century when it was written as a means by which non-schooled converts in Dacia might remember the creed, may be less often used, and its place taken by a

* The eight-day, or outdooring, ceremony takes place in every Akan home eight days after birth. The child is named and welcomed into the society of the present and the past. (See also page 129.)

new Te Deum putting in the form of a Fante lyric the essentials of the faith this generation in Ghana needs to remember. We say 'less often used', for there is loss as well as gain—as is well illustrated by the tension within the Catholic Church over the use of Latin in public worship—for without such common forms of expression the followers of Christ from every country and continent may be dumb and feel estranged in one another's company.

Whatever may be the national grouping of these local fellowships, it will be led by Africans. The day of the overseas missionary in the numbers of the past and the present will very soon be over. Visas will be restricted: an action not necessarily to be ascribed to a breach of the freedom to worship and propagate one's faith; it may prove necessary for a number of reasons, not least the implacable alliance of some missionaries with their own culture and nationality. This emphasises how necessary it is that those expatriate technicians who still serve Africa should take their natural place in the local fellowship. A cutting off of missionaries could, like localised forms of worship, militate against recognition of the world-wide nature of the Church. In every land there is need to counter-balance those forces which take local patriotism and put it on a pedestal in its own right, rather than using it to form the basis of a wider loyalty to all mankind. There is a necessary place for international teams in the service and mission of the Church, for the local Christian fellowship must always witness to the one-ness in Christ of all mankind. Such teams will have to be genuinely international in composition and operation, in Port Sunlight, Cheshire, as well as in Port Harcourt, Nigeria; in Livingston, Scotland, as well as in Livingstone, Zambia.

With the contribution from outside thus reduced to those proportions which should pertain in every country which believes in the community of nations, the Church in Africa will throb more rhythmically to the life of the African conti-

nent. Its vitality will be kept fresh and vigorous through
the life given it by the Spirit of God, both within its fellowship
and as its members meet the rough warm strength of human
activity in every part of the nation. For Christian and non-
Christian, the Church and the world, national and international, divine and human, are held in tension throughout this
life right up to the gates of death; for we too are 'convinced that
there is nothing in death or life, in the realm of spirits or super-
human powers, in the world as it is or the world as it shall be,
in the forces of the universe, in heights or depths—nothing in
all creation that can separate us from the love of God in Christ
Jesus our Lord'.[5]

APPENDICES

I

Statistical Notes

1. AFRICAN INDEPENDENT CHURCHES

It is difficult to estimate the total number of members of the Independent
Churches throughout the continent. The most reliable figures are for the
Republic of South Africa. The 1960 census there gave 2,188,303 Indepen-
dents out of a total of 7,258,187 African Christians. Comparison in previous
censuses with the largest of the historic Churches among Africans, the
Methodist with 1,313,129 African members, indicates a slight relative
regression in that Church and a rapid advance in the Independent
Churches. The respective figures for 1946, 1951 and 1960 are: Methodist
percentage of total African population: 12·9, 12·2, 12·0; Independent
Churches: 9·6, 18·6, 20·1.

Elsewhere their numbers are smaller. In Kenya, the Independent
Churches claim some 500,000 adherents out of a total Christian community
of about 5 million. More detailed figures for Kenya, as for other countries,
are expected to be available in 1967 as the result of the work of the Research
Unit of the Anglican Church in Nairobi.

An estimate of 'actively connected' Independents in Nigeria is put by
competent observers at 225,000. This figure corresponds to official returns
in other Churches, rather than to the larger number in census returns.

The 1960 census figures for Ghana give the religion of those over fifteen
years old. Making a proportionate allowance for children, we have 175,000
Independents out of a total of 2,900,000 Christians.

2. THE DIFFERENCES BETWEEN CENSUS AND CHURCH RETURNS

A comparison in respect of three countries between available census figures
and the number of Catholics and catechumens claimed by the Roman

Catholic Church shows that the number the Church recognises is considerably less than those who themselves claim Roman Catholic allegiance. In South Africa (1960), 18 per cent more claimed allegiance than the official Church records claimed. In Ghana (1960), after making allowance for the census tables for religion being for those over fifteen, the figure is 38 per cent. In Kenya (1962), it is 45 per cent. An even greater discrepancy appears in Protestant figures. In Ghana, the Protestant Church returns for 1960 show 804,918, including children. The census, of those over fifteen, shows 1,096,711: a figure which, if reflected proportionately among children, becomes 1,975,684. This is more than double the Church returns, in fact 145 per cent in excess. In Kenya (1962), Church returns are about 900,000 whereas the census gives 2,896,900 Protestants: an excess of 220 per cent.

3. ESTIMATES OF THE TOTALS OF THE THREE MAJOR RELIGIOUS COMMUNITIES

J. C. Froelich in 1962 assessed the position as: total population south of the Sahara, 200 million; Animists, 117 million; Muslims, 50 million; Christians, 33 million. (Article in *Outre-mer*, January 1963.)

The *World Map of Religions and Missions*, in its 4th edition 1966, quotes 1963 figures; total population 181 million; Christians, 44 million—of whom Roman Catholics 23 million, Protestants 17 million and Ethiopian Orthodox 4 million. (Published by Evangelischer Missionsverlag, Stuttgart; English edition from Edinburgh House Press, London.)

The estimate on page 22 has been arrived at as follows. United Nations reference gives the total population of sub-Saharan Africa in 1966 as 230 million. Several sources give an approximation for Muslims between 50 and 55 million. The *World Christian Handbook* figure (published 1962) for total Protestants is recorded by their Churches as $17\frac{1}{2}$ million. An allowance of 30 per cent for the difference between Church and individual claims would increase this $17\frac{1}{2}$ million to $22\frac{3}{4}$. Similarly for Catholics, a 1963 Church figure of 24 million, with a rather smaller differential, would become 27 million. Ethiopian Orthodox are probably about 10 million. This would leave the remainder, some 115 million, to be classified as Animists. It may well be that the census figures have to be interpreted as meaning that, over the whole of the region, there are several million thus classified as Animists who in fact claim to be Christians. An urgent responsibility rests on the Churches for incorporating these men and women into the Christian fellowship.

II

Distribution of the Churches in Sub-Saharan Africa

While it is hoped that this list will be of use for reference, its purpose is to indicate a pattern rather than to be a directory.

ANGLICAN PROVINCES (number of dioceses in brackets)

South Africa: South Africa (11), Lesotho, Mozambique, Swaziland
West Africa: Gambia and Rio Pongas, Sierra Leone, Ghana, Nigeria (7)
Central Africa: Rhodesia (2), Malawi, Zambia
East Africa: Kenya (4), Tanzania (4)
Uganda: Uganda (7), Rwanda, Burundi
Missionary Dioceses: Madagascar, Mauritius, Sudan

ASSEMBLIES OF GOD (Pentecostal)

Chad, Congo-Kinshasa, Ethiopia, Ghana, Ivory Coast, Kenya, Lesotho, Liberia, Malawi, Mali, Mozambique, Nigeria, Rhodesia, Sierra Leone, South Africa, Swaziland, Tanzania, Togo, Uganda, Upper Volta, Zambia

BAPTIST

Angola, Burundi, Cameroon, Central African Republic, Chad, Congo-Kinshasa, Congo-Brazzaville, Ethiopia, Ghana, Ivory Coast, Kenya, Liberia, Malawi, Mali, Mozambique, Nigeria, Rhodesia, Rwanda, Senegal, Sierra Leone, South Africa, Tanzania, Uganda, Zambia.

CHRISTIAN AND MISSIONARY ALLIANCE

Congo-Kinshasa, Gabon, Guinea, Ivory Coast, Mali, Upper Volta

CHURCH OF THE BRETHREN

Central African Republic, Nigeria

CHURCH OF GOD

Kenya, Nigeria

CHURCH OF THE NAZARENE

Central African Republic, Malawi, Mozambique, Rhodesia, Swaziland, South Africa, Zambia

CONGREGATIONAL

Botswana, Madagascar, Rhodesia, Sierra Leone, South Africa, South West Africa, Zambia

DISCIPLES OF CHRIST

Congo-Kinshasa, Malawi, South Africa, Zambia

DUTCH REFORMED

Nederduits Gereformeerde: Botswana, Malawi, Rhodesia, South Africa, South West Africa, Zambia
Gereformeerde: South Africa
Nederduits Hervormde: South Africa

ETHIOPIAN ORTHODOX CHURCH

Ethiopia

EVANGELICAL UNITED BRETHREN

Nigeria, Sierra Leone

LUTHERAN (in brackets, number of synods or independent church groups)

Cameroon (2), Central African Republic, Ethiopia, Ghana, Kenya, Liberia, Madagascar, Nigeria (2), Rhodesia, South Africa (10), South West Africa (3), Tanzania (7), Zambia

[166]

Appendix II

MENNONITE

Congo-Kinshasa, Ethiopia, Ghana, Nigeria, Somalia, Tanzania

METHODIST

Conferences (number of districts in brackets): Angola (3), Congo-Kinshasa
—*Central* (11), *Southern* (9), Ghana (5), Ivory Coast, Kenya (2), Liberia
(11), Mozambique-South Africa (7), Nigeria (7), Rhodesia (3) and (4),
Sierra Leone (2), South Africa (8)
Districts: Dahomey (with Togo), Gambia
African Methodist Episocpal: Botswana, Ghana, Lesotho, Liberia, Nigeria,
Sierra Leone, South Africa, Swaziland
African Methodist Episcopal Zion: Ghana, Liberia, Nigeria

MISSION COVENANT CHURCH OF SWEDEN AND EVANGELICAL
COVENANT CHURCH (USA)

Congo-Brazzaville, Congo-Kinshasa

MORAVIAN

South Africa, Tanzania

PLYMOUTH BRETHREN (Christian Missions in Many Lands)

Angola, Central African Republic, Chad, Congo-Kinshasa, Sierra
Leone, Tanzania, Zambia

REFORMED AND PRESBYTERIAN

Cameroon, Central African Republic, Congo-Kinshasa, Dahomey,
Ethiopia, Gabon, Ghana, Kenya, Lesotho, Liberia, Malawi, Mozambique, Nigeria, Rhodesia, South Africa, Togo

ROMAN CATHOLIC

Archdioceses (number of dioceses in brackets): Angola (Luanda 4);
Burundi (Gitega 3); Cameroon (Yaoundé 7); Central African Republic
(Bangui 3); Chad (Fort Lamy 3); Congo-Brazzaville (2); Congo-
Kinshasa (Kinshasa 8, Mbandaka 6, Lubumbashi 5, Luluaborg 3,
Kisangani 7, Bukavu 5); Dahomey (Cotonou 4); Ethiopia (Asmara,
Gimma, Harar); Gabon (Libreville); Ghana (Cape Coast 6); Guinea
(Conakry 2); Ivory Coast (Abidjan 5); Kenya (Nairobi 7); Lesotho
(Maseru 2); Malagasy (Tananarive 4, Diego Suarez 4, Fianarantsoa 4);

Malawi (Blantyre 4); Mali (Bamako 3); Mozambique (Lourenço Marques 7); Nigeria (Lagos 5, Kaduna 5, Onitsha 7); Rhodesia (Salisbury 4); Rwanda (Kabgayi 3); Senegal (Dakar); South Africa (Bloemfontein 4, Cape Town 4, Durban 5, Pretoria 2); Tanzania (Dar-es-Salaam 4, Mahengi 4, Tabora 8); Togo (Lome); Uganda (Rubaga 7); Upper Volta (Ougadougou 6); Zambia (Lusaka 7)
Dioceses: Botswana, Gambia, Portuguese Guinea, Spanish Guinea, Liberia, Niger, Sierra Leone, South West Africa, Swaziland

SALVATION ARMY

Territories: Central Africa (Rhodesia, Zambia: HQ Salisbury); Congo (HQ Kinshasa); East Africa (Kenya, Tanzania, Uganda: HQ Nairobi); Equatorial Africa (HQ Brazzaville); Ghana (HQ Accra); Nigeria (HQ Lagos); South Africa (South Africa, Mozambique: HQ Johannesburg)

SEVENTH-DAY ADVENTISTS

Angola, Cameroon, Congo-Kinshasa, Ethiopia, Gambia, Ghana, Ivory Coast, Kenya, Liberia, Madagascar, Malawi, Mali, Mozambique, Nigeria, Rhodesia, Sierra Leone, South Africa, South West Africa, Swaziland, Tanzania, Uganda, Zambia

SOCIETY OF FRIENDS (Quakers)

Burundi, Kenya, Rhodesia, South Africa, Tanzania

UNITED CHURCH OF CANADA

Supports related Churches in Angola, Congo-Kinshasa, Kenya, Zambia

UNITED CHURCH OF CHRIST (USA)

Angola, Ghana, Mozambique, Rhodesia, South Africa, Togo, Zambia

UNITED CHURCH OF ZAMBIA

Uniting Congregational, Evangelical, Methodist and Presbyterian

CHURCHES RELATED TO INTERDENOMINATIONAL MISSIONARY SOCIETIES

African Evangelical Fellowship: Angola, Malawi, Rhodesia, South Africa, Swaziland, Zambia

Appendix II

African Inland Mission: Central African Republic, Congo-Kinshasa, Kenya, Sudan, Tanzania, Uganda
Evangelical Alliance Mission: Rhodesia, South Africa
Regions Beyond Missionary Union: Congo-Kinshasa
Sudan Interior Mission: Dahomey, Ethiopia, Ghana, Liberia, Niger, Nigeria, Somalia, Sudan, Upper Volta
Sudan United Mission: Cameroon, Chad, Nigeria
Unevangelized Fields Mission: Congo-Kinshasa
Worldwide Evangelization Crusade: Congo-Kinshasa, Ghana, Ivory Coast, Liberia, Mali, Portuguese Guinea, Senegal Spanish Guinea, Upper Volta

AFRICAN INDEPENDENT CHURCHES

The list so far given is incomplete without the African Independent Churches. Over 2,000 names could be given for South Africa alone, some consisting of a single congregation, others with a large membership. It has not been possible to list them. This note is a reminder of the gap.

III

The All-Africa Conference of Churches

Following the World Missionary Conference at Edinburgh in 1910, the International Missionary Council was formed. This was an association of two types of National Council: National Councils of Missionary Societies or Mission Boards in Europe, America, Australia; and National Christian Councils in the countries of the so-called 'younger Churches' in Asia, Latin America and Africa. When the World Council of Churches came into being in 1948, conversations took place between these two world bodies, the wcc and the imc, which led to their integration at New Delhi in 1961. Much of the responsibility formerly carried by the imc is now under the care of the Commission on World Mission and Evangelism of the wcc.

Within Africa, the first consultations between the Protestant denominations were at the national level and, in the beginning, between missionaries. Then as Missions gave place to Churches, these Missionary Conferences gave place to Christian Councils—as in Zambia, for example, where the General Missionary Conference of Northern Rhodesia, founded in 1914 with the late Edwin W. Smith as its chairman, became in 1944 the Christian Council of Northern Rhodesia. The Christian Council of Ghana was formed in 1929; that of Kenya in 1942.

On a continent-wide basis, consultation was almost non-existent. When it did happen it took place outside Africa. For most parts of Africa, external links in this century have been not with immediate neighbours but with some centre abroad: Paris, New York or London. It was still the case in the 1950s that more leading Nigerians had been in New York than in Accra, more leading Kenyans in London than in Dar-es-Salaam, more leading Ivoreans in Paris than in Cotonou. At the Jerusalem Conference of the imc in 1928, only five African countries were represented, and of the seven representatives only two were Africans—both of them, significantly, laymen.

Even when the IMC had called a special conference on Africa two years earlier at Le Zoute in Belgium, of the 79 members representing 17 African countries, 72 were missionaries and only 7 Africans. (See report edited by E. W. Smith: *The Christian Mission in Africa*, IMC, 1926.) The balance was improved at the IMC Tambaram Conference in 1938: 17 countries, 18 missionaries, 17 Africans. When, therefore, the first All-Africa Christian Conference met at Ibadan in January 1958, it could claim to be 'a much more widely representative gathering of Africans than had ever before come together for any purpose', for it represented all the major Protestant Churches from 25 countries, and only 48 of the 144 representatives were missionaries.*

At the Ibadan Conference in 1958, 'for the first time the African Church found its voice' under the chairmanship of Sir Francis Ibiam of Nigeria. The subjects discussed within the general theme "The Church in Changing Africa" were: the Church, Youth and Family; the Church and Economic Life; the Church and Citizenship; the Church and Culture; the Growing Church. Findings published under these heads were not spectacular; rather, they marked out the areas in which study and thought were required. The emphasis made by Christians present at Ibadan bore fruit in specific consultations and conferences on an all-Africa basis in following years: Urban Africa (Nairobi 1961), Literature and Audio-Visual (Mindolo 1961), Youth (Nairobi 1962), Education (Salisbury 1962), Independent Church Movements (Mindolo 1962), Home and Family Life (Mindolo 1963), Women's Status and Responsibility in Church and Society (Kampala 1963). These were drawn together again in the General Conference at Kampala in 1963, to lead on to specific subjects again: the Christian Response to the African Revolution—Service, Refugees, International Affairs (Enugu 1965), the Evangelisation of West and Equatorial Africa (Yaoundé 1965), Biblical Revelation and African Beliefs, a conference of African theologians (Ibadan 1966), the Christian Presence in the University (Accra 1966), Lay Training (Mindolo 1964), the Role of Christian Laymen (Yaoundé 1965).

When the Ibadan Conference of January 1958 drew to a close, the participants were of one mind that they must continue the discussion and fellowship they had been experiencing. They therefore passed the following resolution:

In view of the unanimous conviction of this All-Africa Church Conference that the Conference has been of immense value as a means of

* The first African YMCA Conference (Accra 1953) was limited to West and Central Africa, and had 32 representatives from 12 countries. The first All-Africa Lutheran Conference (Marangu 1955) was representative of one Protestant tradition only and of eight countries. The first All-Africa Conference of Teachers Associations (Kampala 1960) was attended by over 90 leaders of teachers' organisations from 20 countries. The first All-Africa Peoples' Conference (Accra, December 1958) represented 28 countries.

fellowship and understanding between the churches in this vast continent, and in view of the many important issues raised and recommendations made in the course of the meetings, be it

Resolved, That this Conference name a committee here to consult with the Christian Councils of Africa, church bodies and other agencies concerned with the witness for Christ in Africa, in order to give consideration to the implementation of the report of this Conference and particularly as to the appointment of a Continuation Committee and/or a regional secretary.

The Continuation, or Provisional Committee as it was sometimes called, was of ten members (six from English-speaking, three from French-speaking and one from Portuguese-speaking countries): Sir Francis Ibiam (Nigeria), Chairman; Mrs E. L. Coker (Sierra Leone); Pasteur J. Keller (Cameroon); Pasteur J. Lubakulu (Belgian Congo); Mr H. Makulu (Northern Rhodesia); Mr J. Miguel (Angola); Bishop S. Moshi (Tanganyika); Dr Alan Paton (South Africa); Dr G. W. Carpenter (United States); Pasteur T. Rasendrahashina (Madagascar). Seven of the major Protestant Churches were represented in this membership: Presbyterian, Anglican, Reformed, Baptist, Congregational, Methodist, Lutheran.

This Continuation Committee became the nucleus committee of the All-Africa Conference of Churches. In September 1959, Dr D. S. G. M'Timkulu —formerly Lecturer in Education at Fort Hare University, South Africa— was appointed Secretary. Under his guidance the series of consultations following Ibadan were organised and the subject matter of their discussion drawn up. It was Dr M'Timkulu who was responsible for guiding the Continuation Committee to lay the foundation for a more firmly established means of relationship between Churches and Christian Councils throughout Africa and so to call the successor conference to Ibadan, at Kampala in April 1963, where the All-Africa Conference of Churches was formally constituted. His colleague in this work, the Associate Secretary, the Reverend James Lawson of Dahomey, has strengthened and sustained the fellowship of African Christians across anglophone and francophone boundaries. When the Kampala Conference came to appoint a continuing committee, the General Committee of the All-Africa Conference of Churches, there were twenty members, of whom fourteen were ordained and six lay, three of these being women. They came from fourteen different countries. A new General Secretary was appointed, Mr S. H. Amissah of Ghana (PO Box 20301, Nairobi, Kenya), with the Reverend J. Lawson continuing as Associate (BP 34, Cotonou, Republic of Dahomey). The AACC publishes a Bulletin three times a year, in English and French editions.

For AACC conferences to be adequately representative of continental thought, a balance had to be sought between men and women and between those from anglophone and francophone countries. These figures for the conferences mentioned above, for representatives as distinct from consultants, were:

	Men	Women	Anglo-phone	Franco-phone	Portu-guese
General Conference, Ibadan 1958:	80 (83%)	16 (17%)	74 (77%)	20 (21%)	2 (2%)
Urban Africa, Nairobi 1961:	15 (94%)	1 (6%)	9 (56%)	7 (44%)	—
Literature, Mindolo 1961:	24 (100%)	—	19 (79%)	5 (21%)	—
Youth, Nairobi 1962:	289 (76%)	92 (24%)	287 (75%)	94 (25%)	—
Education, Salisbury 1962:	39 (80%)	10 (20%)	35 (71%)	14 (29%)	—
Home & Family Life, Mindolo 1963:	15 (43%)	20 (57%)	18 (51%)	17 (49%)	—
General Conference, Kampala 1963:	116 (79%)	30 (21%)	96 (66%)	50 (34%)	—
Inter-Church Aid, Enugu 1965:	50 (85%)	9 (15%)	38 (64%)	20 (34%)	1 (2%)

In the general conferences, the proportion of francophone participants has increased. An estimate of the relative Protestant populations suggests a francophone figure of 27 per cent. In a conference limited in numbers, a balance has to be struck between a representative for every denomination in each country and strict representation according to size. The latter is not possible; for example, the African members alone of the Methodist Church in South Africa are more in number than all the Protestants in Cameroon. The 34 per cent francophone membership of both Kampala and Enugu would seem to be a reasonable balance. There is still need on both sides for greater appreciation of differences in tradition and modes of expression reflected in these two metropolitan languages; and, as in Europe, it is more often the anglophones who think everyone else should understand them.

The ratio of women to men was only once truly reflected, in the Home and Family Life Seminar in which the basis of invitation was married couples. In all other cases, as in Church conferences elsewhere, the number of women is small. Even so it is better than often occurs in the West. So long as the chief theologians and administrators of the Church are ordained, the average Church conference will be composed of more ministers than laymen; so long as the ordained ministry is restricted to men, this automatically reserves for them more than 50 per cent of conference places. Very seldom do lay places reflect the relative number of men and women in the congregations. The chances of women forming more than 25 per cent of a general Church conference are therefore very low. That Ibadan achieved 17 per cent and Kampala 21 per cent is a hopeful augury, though this was not through the deliberate act of member Churches so much as through the reservation of a number of places in the planning of the conferences. A glance at the names of those women present suggests that what they lacked in numbers they made up in personality; they were there in their own right, not because their office could not be overlooked.

IV

Organisations of Christian Co-operation in Africa

ALL-AFRICA CONFERENCE OF CHURCHES

General Secretary: PO Box 20301, Nairobi, Kenya
Associate General Secretary: BP 34, Cotonou, Dahomey
Ecumenical Programme for Emergency Action in Africa: PO Box 20301, Nairobi, Kenya
Education Secretaries: PO Box 3248, Ibadan, Nigeria
Home and Family Life Secretary: PO Box 20301, Nairobi, Kenya
Literature Clearing House (English-speaking countries): PO Box 1319, Kitwe, Zambia
Centre de Littérature Evangélique (French-speaking countries): BP 1133, Yaoundé, Cameroon
Africa Literature Centre (Writing and Art Schools): PO Box 1319, Kitwe, Zambia
Youth Secretary: PO Box 1131, Kitwe, Zambia
Broadcasting and Visual Aids Secretary: PO Box 14206, Nairobi, Kenya
Broadcasting and Visual Aids Associate Secretary: PO Box 67, Ilesha, Nigeria

ASSOCIATION OF EVANGELICALS OF AFRICA AND MADAGASCAR

Central Office: PO Box 9332, Nairobi, Kenya

CATHOLIC SECRETARIATS

There is no general African office of the Roman Church. Secretariats in each country can be addressed c/o of the Archbishop's House at the country's capital. (See list of archdioceses on page 167.)

[177]

Education: Catholic International Education Office (Regional Secretariat for Africa and Madagascar), PO Box 2149, Brazzaville, Congo-Brazzaville

CHRISTIAN COUNCILS

Angola: CP 1223C, Luanda
Burundi: BP 17, Usumbura
Cameroon: BP 491, Yaoundé
Congo-Kinshasa, BP 3094, Kinshasa-Kalina
Ethiopia: PO Box 2642, Addis Ababa
Ghana: PO Box 919, Accra
Kenya: PO Box 5009, Nairobi
Madagascar, c/o Temple d'Ambatovinaky, Tananarive
Malawi, PO Box 413, Blantyre
Mozambique, CP 21, Lourenço Marques
Nigeria, PMB 2838, Lagos
Rhodesia, PO Box 904, Salisbury
Rwanda, BP 79, Kigali
Sierra Leone, PO Box 404, Freetown
South Africa, PO Box 2846, Cape Town
Tanzania, PO Box 2537, Dar-es-Salaam
Uganda, PO Box 2886, Kampala
Zambia, PO Box 315, Lusaka

BIBLE SOCIETIES (translation, publishing and distribution)

Cameroon (including Gabon): BP 1133, Yaoundé
Central African Republic (including Chad and Congo-Brazzaville): BP 1127, Bangui
Congo-Kinshasa: BP 8911, Kinshasa
East Africa (Kenya, Mauritius, Tanzania and Uganda): PO Box 12983, Nairobi, Kenya
Ethiopia (including French Somaliland and Somalia): PO Box 130, Addis Ababa
French-speaking West Africa (Dahomey, Guinea, Ivory Coast, Mali, Niger, Senegal, Togo and Upper Volta): BP 1529, Abidjan, Ivory Coast
Ghana: PO Box 761, Accra
Liberia: PO Box 39, Monrovia
Madagascar: BP 922, Tananarive
Malawi: PO Box 740, Blantyre
Mozambique: Casa da Biblia, Av. Pinheiro Chagas 2678, Lourenço Marques
Nigeria: PO Box 68, Apapa

Appendix IV

Rhodesia: PO Box 1081, Salisbury
Sierra Leone: PO Box 1169, Freetown
South Africa (including Botswana, Lesotho and Swaziland): PO Box 215, Cape Town
Sudan: PO Box 532, Khartoum
Zambia: PO Box 1668, Kitwe

GENERAL

All-Africa Church Music Association: PO Box 636 E, Salisbury, Rhodesia
Christian Institute of Southern Africa: 408, Dunwell, 35, Jorissen St, Brammfontein, Johannesburg
Islam in Africa Committee (including Pierre Benignus Study Centre): PO Box 4045, Ibadan, Nigeria
Mindolo Ecumenical Foundation: PO Box 1192, Kitwe, Zambia
Society for African Church History (Secretary): Dr W. O. Ajaye, Dept. of Comparative Religion, University of Ife, Nigeria
World Student Christian Federation (Africa Secretary): PO Box 1756, Kitwe, Zambia

PUBLICATIONS

All-Africa Conference of Churches Bulletin (Subscriptions): PO Box 1319, Kitwe, Zambia
Urban Africa Bulletin: PO Box 1046, Monrovia, Liberia
African Ecclesiastical Review: PO Box 232, Masaka, Uganda
Revue du Clergé Africain: Mayidi, Inkisi BP 6, Kinshasa, Congo-Kinshasa
Documentation et Information Africaines: BP 2598, Kinshasa, Congo-Kinshasa
Ministry: PO Box 32, Morija, Lesotho
Flambeau: BP 1133, Yaoundé, Cameroon

RELATED ORGANISATIONS OUTSIDE AFRICA

Division of Inter-Church Aid, Refugee and World Service, World Council of Churches, 150 Route de Ferney, Geneva 20, Switzerland; Division of World Mission and Evangelism—address as above

Canada: Canadian Council of Churches, 40 St Clair Avenue East, Toronto 7
Denmark: Dansk Missionraad (Danish Missionary Council), Nørregade 11, Copenhagen K;
Church of Denmark Inter-Church Aid Committee—address as above
France: Secours Catholique, 120 Rue de Cherche-Midi, Paris 6;
Société des Missions Evangéliques de Paris, 102 Boulevard Argo, Paris 14

Germany: "Bread for the World", Gerokstrasse 21, Postfach 476, Stuttgart;
IMJEKD—address as above;
Deutscher Evangelischer Missions-Rat (German Missionary Council), Mittelweg 143, Hamburg 13;
Misereor (German Bishops' Fund), Mozartstrasse 11, Aachen
Italy: Caritas Internationalis, Via della Conciliazione 15, Rome
Netherlands: Dutch Committee for Inter-Church Aid, Cornelis Houtmanstraat 17, Utrecht;
Nederlandsche Zendingsraad (Dutch Missionary Council), Prins Hendriklaan 37, Amsterdam 7
Sweden: Svenska Missionsradet (Swedish Missionary Council), Tegnergatan 8, Stockholm Va;
Swedish Inter-Church Aid Committee, Nordiska Ekumenish Institutet, Sigtuna
Switzerland: Caritas, Rue de Cornevin 11, Geneva;
Conseil Suisse des Missions Evangéliques (Swiss Missionary Council), Rue de Genève 49, 1225 Chêne-Bourg, Geneva;
Hilfswerk der Evangelischen Kirchen der Schweiz (HEKS), Stampfenbachstrasse 123, Zürich
United Kingdom: Africa Secretary, Conference of Missionary Societies in Great Britain and Ireland, 2 Eaton Gate, London S.W.1;
Catholic Overseas Appointments, 38 King Street, London W.C.2;
Christian Aid, British Council of Churches, 10 Eaton Gate, London S.W.1;
Mission Secretariat (Catholic), St Joseph's College, London N.W.7;
Overseas Appointments Bureau, Christian Education Movement, 38 King Street, London W.C.2
United States: Africa Department, Division of Overseas Ministries, National Council of Churches of Christ in the United States of America, 475 Riverside Drive, New York, N.Y., 10027;
Catholic Relief Service, Empire State Building, New York 1, N.Y.

SELECT BIBLIOGRAPHY

Select Bibliography

Other works of more special interest will be found cited, with publication details, in the References section.

HISTORY OF THE CHURCH IN AFRICA

GERDENER, G. B. A., *Recent Developments in the South African Mission Field*, Marshall, Morgan and Scott, London 1958.

GROVES, C. P., *The Planting of Christianity in Africa*, Vols. I–IV, Lutterworth Press, London 1948, 1954, 1955, 1958.

KITTLER, G. D., *The White Fathers*, Allen and Unwin, London 1957; Doubleday, New York 1961.

NEILL, S., *A History of Christian Missions*, Penguin, Harmondsworth, Middlesex and Baltimore, Md., 1964.

OLIVER, R., *The Missionary Factor in East Africa*, Longmans, London, 2nd edn, 1965.

PLESSIS, J. du, *Christian Missions in South Africa*, Longmans, London 1911.

TODD, J. M., *African Mission*, Burns and Oates, London 1962.

WARREN, M., *The Missionary Movement from Britain in Modern History*, Student Christian Movement Press, London 1965.

INDIGENOUS AFRICAN RELIGIONS

FIELD, M. J., *Search for Security*, Faber, London 1960; Northwestern University Press, Evanston 1960.

PARRINDER, E. G., *West African Religion*, Epworth Press, London 1961.

SMITH, E. W. and PARRINDER, E. G. (eds), *African Ideas of God*, Edinburgh House Press, London, 2nd edn, 1961.

TAYLOR, J. V., *The Primal Vision*, Student Christian Movement Press, London 1963; Fortress Press, Philadelphia 1964.

TEMPELS, P., *La Philosophie bantoue*, Présence Africaine, Paris 1949; published in English as *Bantu Philosophy* (trans. King, C.), Présence Africaine, Paris 1952.

ISLAM

FISHER, H. J., *Ahmadiyyah*, Oxford University Press, London and New York, 1963.

FROELICH, J. C., *Les Musulmans d'Afrique noire*, Editions de l'Orante, Paris 1962.

MONTEIL, V., *L'Islam noir*, Editions de l'Orante, Paris 1964.

TRIMINGHAM, J. S., *The Christian Church and Islam in West Africa*, Student Christian Movement Press, London 1955; Friendship Press, New York 1955.

—— *Islam in West Africa*, Oxford University Press, London and New York, 1959.

—— *A History of Islam in West Africa*, Oxford University Press, London and New York, 1962.

—— *Islam in East Africa*, Oxford University Press, London and New York, 1964.

CHRISTIANITY, AFRICAN CULTURE AND RELIGIOUS THOUGHT

DEBRUNNER, H., *A Church Between Colonial Powers*, Lutterworth Press, London 1965; Allenson, Napierville, Ill., 1965.

IDOWU, E. B., *Towards an Indigenous Church*, Oxford University Press, London and New York, 1965.

LEDOGAR, R. (ed), *Katigondo: Presenting the Christian Message to Africa*, Chapman and Hall, London 1965.

MULLIN, J., *The Catholic Church in Modern Africa*, Geoffrey Chapman, London 1965.

TAYLOR, J. V., *The Growth of the Church in Buganda*, Student Christian Movement Press, London 1958; Friendship Press, New York 1958.

—— and LEHMANN, D., *Christians of the Copperbelt*, Student Christian Movement Press, London 1961; Friendship Press, New York 1961.

WEMAN, H., *African Music and the Church in Africa*, Swedish Institute of Missionary Research, Stockholm 1960.

WILLIAMSON, S. G., *Akan Religion and the Christian Faith*, Ghana Universities Press, Accra 1965.

Christianity and African Culture, Christian Council of the Gold Coast (Ghana), Accra 1955.

Des Prêtres noirs s'interrogent, Editions du Cerf, Paris 1956.

Select Bibliography

CHRISTIANITY AND POLITICAL, ECONOMIC AND SOCIAL ISSUES

ABRECHT, P., *The Churches and Rapid Social Change*, Student Christian Movement Press, London 1961.

BEAVER, R. P. (ed), *Christianity and African Education*, Eerdmans, Grand Rapids, Michigan 1966.

DOHERTY, M. A. (ed), *The Role of the African Woman*, A Report of Catholic Seminars and study weeks, Africa Centre, London 1963.

MARIOGHAE, M. and FERGUSON, J., *Nigeria Under the Cross*, Highway Press, London 1965.

PAYNE, D. (ed), *African Independence and Christian Freedom*, Oxford University Press, London and New York, 1965.

PHILLIPS, A. (ed), *Survey of African Marriage and Family Life*, Oxford University Press, London and New York, 1953.

WELBOURN, F. B., *East African Christian*, Oxford University Press, London and New York, 1965.

All-Africa Seminar on the Christian Home and Family Life, World Council of Churches, Geneva 1963.

Catholic Education in the Service of Africa, Report of the Kinshasa Conference, Catholic International Education Office, Brazzaville 1966.

Christian Education in Africa, Report of the Salisbury Conference, Oxford University Press, London 1963.

Christian Responsibility in an Independent Nigeria, Christian Council of Nigeria, Lagos 1962.

Pastoral Letters of Catholic Bishops: *The Catholic Church in an Independent Nigeria*, 1960; *Unity and Freedom in the New Tanganyika*, 1960; *Shaping Our National Destiny* (Uganda), 1962.

The Church and Human Relations, Christian Council of Rhodesia, Salisbury, Rhodesia, 1965.

AFRICAN INDEPENDENT CHURCHES

BAETA, C. G., *Prophetism in Ghana*, Student Christian Movement Press, London 1962.

HAYWARD, V. E. W. (ed), *African Independent Church Movements*, Edinburgh House Press, London 1965; Friendship Press, New York 1965.

PAUW, B. A., *Religion in a Tswana Chiefdom*, Oxford University Press, London and New York, 2nd edn, 1961.

SUNDKLER, B. G. M., *Bantu Prophets in South Africa*, Oxford University Press, London and New York, 2nd edn, 1961.

TURNER, H. W., *Profile Through Preaching*, Edinburgh House Press, London 1965.

[185]

TURNER, H. W., *History of An African Independent Church*, 2 vols., Oxford University Press, London and New York, 1967.

WELBOURN, F. B., *East African Rebels*, Student Christian Movement Press, London 1961; Friendship Press, New York 1961.

—— and OGOT, B. A., *A Place to Feel at Home*, Oxford University Press, London and New York, 1966.

References

For works cited here without full publication details, see the Select Bibliography.

New Testament references throughout are to the text of the *New English Bible*.

1. THE QUESTION POSED

   1. D. Webster, Inaugural Lecture as Professor of Missions, Selly Oak Colleges, Birmingham 1966; mimeograph.

2. THE COMING OF CHRISTIANITY TO AFRICA

   1. R. Slade, *King Leopold's Congo*, Oxford University Press, London and New York, 1962, p. 141.

   2. J. F. A. Ajayi, *Christian Missions in Nigeria, 1841–1891*, Longmans, London 1965; Northwestern University Press, Evanston, 1965; ch. 8. J. B. Webster, *The African Churches Among the Yoruba, 1888–1902*, Oxford University Press, London and New York, 1965. F. L. Bartels, *The Roots of Ghana Methodism*, Cambridge University Press, Cambridge and New York, 1965, pp. 138, 137.

   3. Webster, *op. cit.*, pp. 43–4.

   4. *The New Testament*, First Epistle of John, 4, v. 1.

   5. The author was unable to verify this reference by the time the book went to press.

3. WEAKNESS AND STRENGTH OF THE CHURCH

   1. R. Oliver, *The Missionary Factor in East Africa*, 2nd edn, pp. *xi*, 291.

   2. *The New Testament*, First Epistle of Peter, 4, v. 17.

3. S. Neill, *A History of Christian Missions*, p. 530.

4. Oliver, *op. cit.*, p. *x*.

5. C. Hoskyns, *The Congo Since Independence*, Oxford University Press, London and New York, 1965, p. 34.

6. R. Delavignette, *Freedom and Authority in French West Africa*, Oxford University Press, London and New York, 1960, pp. 96, 99.

7. For a short account of this development, see *Christian Education in Africa*, ch. 3.

8. F. D. Harker, *The Church is There* (*in Ghana*), Church of Scotland Foreign Mission Committee, Edinburgh 1964, p. 18.

9. *Report of the Kenya Education Commission*, Part I, Nairobi 1964.

10. Bartels, *op. cit.*, p. 241.

11. Cf. K. Little, *West African Urbanization*, Cambridge University Press, Cambridge and New York, 1965, ch. 2.

12. A. Hastings, *The Pattern of African Mission Work*, Africa Centre leaflet, London 1963, ch. 2.

13. B. G. M. Sundkler, *The Christian Ministry in Africa*, Swedish Institute of Missionary Research, Stockholm 1960, p. 315.

14. K. E. Kirk, *The Vision of God*, Longmans, London, 2nd edn 1932, p. 469.

15. H. Debrunner, *A Church Between Colonial Powers*, p. 230.

16. Cf. *Flambeau*, Centre de Littérature Evangélique, Yaoundé, August and November 1965.

17. *The New Testament*, Gospel of St John, 1, v. 14.

18. Ibid, First Epistle of John, 1, v. 1.

19. *Christian Responsibility in an Independent Nigeria*, p. 114.

20. W. M. Macmillan, *Africa Emergent*, Penguin, Harmondsworth, Middlesex, and Baltimore, Md., 1949, p. 61.

21. *Christianity and African Culture*, p. 56.

22. Ibid., p. *iii*.

23. M. J. Field, *Search for Security*.

24. F. B. Welbourn and B. A. Ogot, *A Place to Feel at Home*, p. 128.

25. S. G. Williamson, *Akan Religion and the Christian Faith*, p. 176.

26. Cited in *Christianity and African Culture*, p. *iii*.

27. Neill, *op. cit.*, p. 540.

28. Bartels, *op. cit.*, p. 279.

29. Z. K. Matthews, "Can Christianity Survive in Africa?", *Ministry*, Morija, Lesotho, April 1965, p. 97.

30. Ajayi, *op. cit.*, p. 204*n*.

31. Williamson, *op. cit.*, p. 171*ff*.

32. M. Warren, *The Missionary Movement from Britain in Modern History*, p. 166.

33. *Christianity and African Culture*, p. 56.

34. Ibid., p. 45.

References

4. CHALLENGES FACING THE CHURCH

1. *The New Testament*, Gospel of St John, 8, v. 32.
2. *The Christian Contribution to a Dynamic Society in Tanganyika*, Christian Council, Dar-es-Salaam 1963, p. 7; mimeograph.
3. H. Isaacs, cited in M. Warren, *op. cit.*, p. 126.
4. M. Warren, *op. cit.*, p. 84.
5. E. Ilogu, "The Contribution of the Church to National Unity in Nigeria", *International Review of Missions*, London, July 1964.
6. F. B. Welbourn, *Religion and Politics in Uganda, 1952–62*, East African Publishing House, Nairobi 1965, p. 62.
7. Idem, *East African Rebels*, p. 176.
8. P. Mason, *Prospero's Magic*, Oxford University Press, London and New York, 1963, p. 146.
9. P. D. Devanandan and M. M. Thomas (eds), *Christian Participation in Nation Building*, National Christian Council of India, Bangalore 1960, p. 225.
10. J. S. Annan, article in *Report of Foyer John Knox Seminar*, Geneva 1965; mimeograph.
11. *The New Testament*, Gospel of St Matthew, 6, v. 11; and Gospel of St Luke, 4, v. 4.
12. P. Abrecht, *The Churches and Rapid Social Change*, pp. 118–19.
13. K. A. Busia, in *African Worlds* (ed Daryll Forde), Oxford University Press, London and New York, 1954, p. 191.
14. R. S. Rattray, *Religion and Art in Ashanti*, Oxford University Press, London and New York, 1927, pp. *v–vi*.
15. *The New Testament*, The Epistle to the Hebrews, 11, v. 40.
16. B. Clements, *Philip Cometh to Andrew*, Longmans, London 1930, p. 53.
17. J. V. Taylor, *The Primal Vision*, p. 171.
18. *The Catholic Church in an Independent Nigeria*, Office of the Hierarchy, Lagos 1960, pp. 29–30.
19. Proceedings to be published by the International African Institute.
20. Adapted from R. E. S. Tanner, "Towards an African Catholicism", *Ministry*, Morija, Lesotho, July 1964, p. 167.
21. Cited by T. P. Melady, article in *Race*, Institute of Race Relations, London, October 1965, p. 151.
22. J. V. Taylor, *op. cit.*, p. 115.
23. Idem, *The Growth of the Church in Buganda*, pp. 259–60.
24. Margery Perham, *Lugard: The Years of Authority*, Collins, London 1960; Oxford University Press, New York 1960; pp. 496–511.
25. Ibid., p. 497.
26. Victor Murray, *The School in the Bush*, Longmans, London, 2nd edn, 1938, p. 281. For a statement of the secular standpoint of the administration in the French colonial tradition, see R. Delavignette, *op. cit.*, p. 102*ff.*

27. H. J. Fisher, *Ahmadiyyah*, p. 185.

28. J. B. Taylor, mimeographed report, Selly Oak Colleges, Birmingham 1966.

29. J. C. Froelich, article in *Le mois en Afrique*, Dakar and Paris, January 1966, p. 55.

30. Fisher, *op. cit.*, p. 16.

31. J. S. Trimingham, *A History of Islam in West Africa*, p. 229. In this chapter I am frequently under debt to Trimingham's historical surveys.

32. Idem, *Islam in East Africa*, p. 179; *A History of Islam in West Africa*, p. 233.

33. J. H. S. Crossley, article in *Ministers' Missionary Union Bulletin*, London, May 1965.

34. Trimingham, *The Christian Church and Islam in West Africa*, p. 40.

35. R. M. Jones, in the *Report of the Jerusalem Conference of the International Council*, Oxford University Press, Oxford 1928, Vol. I, p. 284; cited in C. M. West, "Community, Christian and Secular", *Man and Community*, Student Christian Movement Press, London 1966, p. 336.

36. *The New Testament*, Gospel of St John, 10, v. 10.

37. Ibid., First Epistle of Paul to the Corinthians, 3. vv. 22–3.

38. Ibid., Epistle of Paul to the Colossians, 1, v. 16.

39. A. Luthuli, *Let My People Go*, Collins, London 1962; McGraw-Hill, New York 1962; p. 154.

40. A. Aluko, *Christianity and Communism*, Daystar Press, Ibadan 1964, p. 68.

5. THE INTELLECTUAL RESPONSE

1. Cited by Melady, *op. cit.*, p. 154.

2. Abbé Pre-Claude Ngoumou, *Flambeau*, Yaoundé, May 1964 and February 1965.

3. R. Ledogar (ed), *Katigondo: Presenting the Christian Message to Africa*, p. 114.

4. *All-Africa Seminar on the Christian Home and Family Life*, 1963.

5. *Freedom under the Cross*, World Student Christian Federation, Geneva 1963, p. 42.

6. *Consultation Digest*, World Council of Churches, Geneva 1965, p. 21.

7. *The Church in Changing Africa*, International Missionary Council, New York 1958, pp. 57–8.

8. *Drumbeats from Kampala*, Lutterworth Press, London 1963, pp. 61–2.

9. Ibid., p. 61.

10. Ibid., p. 61.

11. *Christians and Race Relations in Southern Africa*, World Council of Churches, 1964, p. 13.

12. Ibid., pp. 14–15.

References

13. *Freedom Under the Cross, op. cit.*, p. 7.
14. *Man in Community, op. cit.*, p. 377.
15. *Consultation Digest, op. cit.*, p. 19.
16. *Drumbeats from Kampala, op. cit.*, p. 50.
17. R. Walsh, in *Christianity and African Education* (ed R. P. Beaver), p. 42.
18. *The Church Meets Life in the Town*, Christian Council of Tanganyika, Dar-es-Salaam 1964.
19. *The New Dimensions of Mission for South Africa Today*, Christian Council of South Africa, Cape Town 1964.

6. THE PRACTICAL RESPONSE

1. *Towards a Better Life: The Role of the Church in Rural Development*, Daystar Press, Ibadan 1966.
2. Ledogar, *op. cit.*, p. 129.

7. THE RESPONSE IN AREAS OF CONFLICT

1. Epistle to Diognetus (c. AD 140), in B. J. Kidd, *Documents Illustrative of the History of the Church*, Society for Promoting Christian Knowledge, London 1920, Vol. I, p. 55.
2. Tertullian (c. AD 197), Kidd, *op. cit.*, p. 144.
3. Athenagoras (c. AD 177), Kidd, *op. cit.*, p. 106.
4. *The Martyrdom of Polycarp* (c. AD 156), Kidd, *op. cit.*, p. 68.
5. C. Morris, *The Hour After Midnight*, Longman, London 1961, p. 115.
6. P. Mason, *Year of Decision*, Oxford University Press, London and New York, 1960, pp. 61–3.
7. J. E. Church, *Forgive Them: The Story of an African Martyr*, Hodder and Stoughton, London 1966.
8. Pastoral Letter of the Catholic Bishops of South Africa, 1966.
9. N. Sithole, *African Nationalism*, Oxford University Press, London and New York, 1959.
10. N. Shamuyarira, *Crisis in Rhodesia*, Deutsch, London 1965; Transatlantic Arts, New York 1966; p. 22.
11. Ibid., p. 145.
12. O. Allison, *A Pilgrim Church's Progress*, Highway Press, London 1966, p. 6.

8. THE FUTURE

1. J. H. R. Moorman, *B. K. Cunningham: A Memoir*, Student Christian Movement Press, London 1947, p. 95.
2. *The New Testament*, First Epistle of John, 1, v. 3.
3. Welbourn and Ogot, *op. cit.*, ch. 15.
4. *The Old Testament*, Exodus 12, v. 26.
5. *The New Testament*, Epistle of Paul to the Romans, 8, vv. 38–9.

INDEX

Index

Index

Burundi, 114, 139
Busia, Prof. K. A., 48, 50, 75

CALABAR, 11, 56
Cameroon, 78, 81, 92, 93, 95, 105, 107, 108, 117, 125, 128, 130
Cape Coast, Ghana, 9, 11, 56
Cape of Good Hope, 9
Caradon, Lord, 116
Carpenter, G. W., 173
Catholic Overseas Appointments, 102, 178
Catholic Relief Agency, 114
Census returns, religions, 22, 163
Central Africa Party, 139
Central African Federation, 138, 139
Central African Republic, 114
Centres for study of Church and Society, 72
Césaire, Aimé, 75
Children's Home, Salisbury, 120
Chilema, 111
Chinamano, J., 146
Christian Councils: Congo Protestant Council, 115; Gambia (with RCs), 124; Ghana, 49, 95, 106, 171; Kenya, 117, 137, 171; Lesotho, 124; Nigeria, 103; Study Institute, 111, 119, Local (Port Harcourt), 122; Rhodesia, 106; South Africa, 106, 124, 128; Tanzania, 116; Uganda (with RCs), 123; Zambia, 171
Christian Institute of Southern Africa, 128, 179
Christian Rural Fellowship, Nigeria, 119
Christianity: and African Traditional Religion, 49–50, 73; and Communism, 88; and Islam, 82–3, 128–9, 131, 157; and racialism, 44–5, 81, 88, 147; and

the ritual of life, 72, 156; and Secularism, 85; secularisation, effect of, 82; and sense of community, 86, 92. (See also Christian, The Church)
Christian: ministry of reconciliation, 140, 146; personal experience, 60–2, 75–6, 153; service, 109–22; rhythm of fellowship, service, 155; witness, 129, 130—in face of death, 140, 142, as leaven, 153, to Muslims, 82–3, 128–31, 147, 157
Christiansborg, Accra, 9, 11
Church, The: autonomy, 25–6, 29–31, 52, 140; discipline, polygamy, 42–3; and education, q.v.; eucharistic life, 41, 51, 153, 155–7; family life, 94–5, 102; as institution, 152–3; lay leadership, 12, 52; local fellowship, 155; social service, 118–20, 122, 137; transmitting the faith, 157; united action, q.v.; urban situations, 40, 102–4, 121–2; widespread in Africa, 50–2; worldwide fellowship, 59–60, 141, 148, 153, 158 (see also Christianity, Churches)
Churches
  I. Protestant (mostly confessional and world-related): African Independent, 7, 8, 19–21, 46, 108, 127–8, 163; African Israel Church (Nineveh), Kenya, 49; Church of the Lord (Aladura), Nigeria, 21; Africa Inland, Kenya, 19; *African Methodist Episcopal*, S. Africa, 128; *Anglican*, 18—Botswana, 123, Gambia, 124, Lesotho, 124, Malawi, 111, Sierra Leone, 10, S. Africa, 144, Tanzania, 124, Lambeth Conference, 25, Provinces, 25; Association of Evangelical Churches of West Africa, 19;

Index

Danquah, J. B., 135
Dar-es-Salaam, 104, 126
Deaths, missionary, 11, 12, 15, 36, 142
de Bresillac, Bp, 11
Debrunner, Rev. H., 43
Delavignette, R., 30
Denominational competition: in schools, 35, 38; in congregations, 36–8
Devlin Commission, 138
Dickson, Rev. K. A. , 75
Dini na Mila, 107
Disunity, 36–8; Evangelical-Liberal tension, 126–7
Division of Inter-Church Aid, World Council of Churches, 114, 116
Division of World Mission and Evangelism, World Council of Churches, 108, 171
Doig, Rev. A., 138
Douala, 105
Dramatisation, 47
Dunwell, Rev. J., 11

EAST AFRICAN Diploma in Theology, 107
East African Revival Movement, 49 n, 137, 152
Economic Problems: planning, 88; school leavers, 68, 96: technical development, 69
Ecumenical Programme for Emergency Action in Africa, 116
Edendale 111
Education: Advisory Committee in Education, 17, 32; All-Africa offices, 177, 178; Appointments Bureaux for teachers, 102, 180; conferences on, Salisbury, Kinshasa, 102; in Muslim regions, 81; industrial schools, 122, 132, 137;

school chapels, 126; school leavers, 68, 96; schools, physical by handicapped, 112, 117; secondary schools, 12, 117—famous names, 56, influence on nation-building, 56, 136; sex education, 95; syllabus for ethical teaching (with Muslims), 128; teacher training colleges, 12, 17; teachers—recruitment, 102, 180, in other employment, 57, 120; universities, *q.v.*
Education and Church, general aspects: period of greatest involvement, 16–17, management, 16, 40; dilemma of priorities, 33; dangers of overburdening, 35–6; denominational competition, 35; number of mission schools, 32; future policy, 102
Elliott Commission on Higher Education, 77
Elmina, Ghana, 9
ELWA, 132
Enugu, 97, 105
Ethiopia, 7, 132
ETLF, 132
Eucharist: breaking of bread, 153, 155–7; the cup, 51, 157; infrequent, 41
Evangelism of West Africa Today, conference, 102, 131
Evaton, 128
Expatriates: pastoral responsibility for, 129; technicians, 158

FACULTÉ DE THÉOLOGIE PROTESTANTE, 108
'Faith and Farm' project, 119
Family Apostolate Movements, 94
Family life, 94–5, 102; family prayer, 4, 55
Fante lyrics, 47, 157

[199]

Index

Muslims, 82, 83, 128-9, 131, 157; ethical instruction syllabus, 128; and indigenous culture, 80-81; and indirect rule, 78-9; Islam in Africa Project, 83; liturgy and ritual, 80; number of Muslims, 22, 164; and secularisation, 82; Sudan, 147; and Traditional Religion, 73; West Africa, 78; White Fathers, 82

Islam in Africa Project, 83

Ivory Coast, 11 n, 47, 79, 92, 105, 117, 130

JERUSALEM CONFERENCE, IMC, 171
Jirapa, 119
Johannesburg, 86
Journalism, training courses, 109, 110

KAMPALA, 47, 97, 102
Kanamuzeyi, Rev. Y., 140
Kano, 78
Karefa-Smart, Mrs R., 85
Katigondo, 125
Katsina, Nigeria, 78
Kaunda, Kenneth, 139
Keller, Rev. J., 173
Kenya, 14, 27, 49 n, 56, 57, 106, 107, 108, 112, 117, 130, 136, 163
Kenya Education Commission, 34
Keswick Convention, 13
Khartoum, 147
Kilimanjaro Christian Medical Centre, 113, 120
Kimbangu, Simon, 21
Kimpese, 108
Kinshasa (Leopoldville), 67, 102
Kiongozi, 107
Kirk, Bp K. E., 43
Knight, Rev. C., 12
Kotto, Rev. J., 91

Kumasi, 10, 74, 124
Kwashiorkor, 112

LAGOS, 56, 79, 81, 86, 105
Lambeth Conference, 25
Laubach, Dr F., 55
Lavigerie, Cardinal, 9, 15
Lawson, Rev. J., 173
Lay Ecumenical Centre, Edendale, 111
Lay evangelists, 14; leaders, 12, 52; preachers, 10, 146; students of theology, 54; witness, 53-4
Lay training centres, 109-111; consultations, 170
Leprosy, 113-4
Lesotho (Basutoland), 92, 107, 124, 131
Le Zoute Conference, 172
Liberia, 9, 79, 105, 132
Limuru, Kenya, 106, 108
Literacy, adult, 4, 55, 109, 110
Literature: and Audio-Visual Conference, 102; Africa Literature Centre, 110, 177; Centre de Litterature Evangelique, 177; Literature Clearing House, 177
Livingstone, David, 13, 139
Livinhac, Fr, 37
Lomé, 105
Lubukalu, J., 173
Lugard, Lord, 78
Luluabourg, 111
Lutheran World Federation, 116, 132
Luthuli, Chief A., 87, 145

MABAOTHANA, Bp E., 124
Macmillan, W. M., 48
Madagascar, 92, 131
Makulu, H., 173
Malawi (Nyasaland), 13, 111, 138

[201]

Index